Is God Calling Me?

Michel Pochet

Is God Calling Me?

New City
London Dublin Edinburgh

First published as *Samuel, Samuel*
by Nouvelle Cité, Paris
© Nouvelle Cité 1985

First published in Great Britain in 1992
by New City
57 Twyford Avenue
London W3 9PZ

Translated by John Daly and Jeremy Hummerstone
© English translation 1992 New City

British Library Cataloguing-in-Publication Data
A catalogue record for this book is
available from the British Library

ISBN 0 904287 43 2

Typeset in Great Britain by
Phoenix Typesetting,
Burley-in-Wharfedale, West Yorkshire
Printed and bound in Great Britain by
BPCC Wheatons Ltd, Exeter, Devon

CONTENTS

INTRODUCTION

Oddly enough, even the one thing we ought to be the world experts on, our own selves, always remains a bit of a mystery. Healthy doses of self-honesty may mean that you have some knowledge of the real you, but for the most part the truth about ourselves is veiled as if by a cloud. Yet we are unable to sit back in our armchairs and remain dumb and do nothing before the mystery. We feel the need to explore it, to find out what there is to know. Not just out of curiosity either. For the more you know about yourself, the better the chance you have of living in such a way as to fulfil your potential. In the end, it is a question of what leads to happiness.

But the search for self-knowledge can be a trap. It can degenerate into self-absorption, a kind of morbid nit-picking at your own soul which stops you engaging with others and the rest of the world.

This need not be the case, however. There are ways of asking the question: who am I? which lead you to meet reality, and from that to learn how to cope with things as they are, not as you imagine them to be. With your feet firmly planted on the ground, you can have a real relationship with everything and everyone outside of yourself. This happens in particular when you answer the question: who am I? after asking it in its most acute form: who am I before God? It is the question of vocation, of your own true self. Only by being faithful to this vocation can you find happiness for yourself and be of real service to others.

Vocation is not about what you have to do. That follows from what you are. An artist paints, a monk prays, a married man loves his wife, a mother cares for her children – all the various kinds and dimensions of calling, in their many, many forms, imply actions, but these depend first of all upon an individual's identity. And since in our true selves we are all made firstly to be in relation to God, the question is a spiritual one of how we are to respond to him in our lives.

Michel Pochet's writing in this book is full of practical suggestions, based on a long experience, of how we can grow in the discovery of our vocation. It is not a scholarly treatise, but a fresh look at this vital topic. Certainly, it is one man's offering of his own point of view, but it is precisely in that originality that the value of the book lies. It is the basis for some very useful comments, ones that are to some extent free of certain traditional preconceptions.

It is very much to be hoped that readers of this book will manage to catch the real meaning of its author, in all its exciting freshness, and come themselves to a realization of their own calling from God. To find your vocation in life is an important step in the most challenging adventure you will ever undertake, the adventure of life.

I
The Last Taboo

I am well aware that taboos are deep-rooted, and I don't expect, singlehanded, to put an end to the last and deadliest of them with this little book. The hold a taboo has over us comes partly from the superstitious fear it inspires, but its main strength is in its apparent indestructibility; if I can make a dent in it I shall have achieved something.

I'm afraid, however, that the attempt may not be welcomed by some parents and teachers – those who sincerely believe that the way to keep young people happy is to keep them ignorant. Nor do I expect to please some others, who know quite well what is wrong but are afraid to give it a name, hunting instead for all sorts of euphemisms as if the matter were too shameful to talk about except in veiled language and by those 'in the know'.

As for myself, you might think my courage would fail me at the task I am undertaking, but it doesn't. I will raise this serious subject no matter how embarrassing it is. I will speak the fateful word which brings a blush to the cheek of the most shameless: 'vocation'.

'But surely you don't mean . . . '

'Yes, I'm afraid so – vocation.'

'Do you mean vocation in the scientific or musical sense?'

'Yes, but not only that.'

'Are you worried about the crisis in vocations? Are you recruiting? Are you trying to fill the gaps in the Church's administration? Couldn't you try the small ads? That might do the trick.'

'No, you're on the wrong track entirely.'

'But isn't God still calling young people to follow him, as we used to believe?'

'He certainly is. I have plenty of evidence that many young people are certain in their heart of hearts that God is calling them personally, but they cannot find words to express what is happening to them. And yet it is the most wonderful thing they will ever experience. Since they can't handle it on their own, they try to tell someone older, and then they meet only scepticism and misunderstanding.'

The various ideas developed here arose out of conversations with young people about their vocations, and this accounts for the general tone of the book. Anyone looking for a closely reasoned study of the subject will be disappointed. But if you are facing the problem of what to do with your future and you believe that God has some part to play in it, you will, I hope, find some useful advice here and be encouraged to press on without being afraid of what others might say.

I make no attempt to set out an argument along classical lines, but I hope this book will not therefore be any less acceptable to parents, teachers and clergy. I hope they will welcome it for what it is intended to be, a help for those in their charge.

The book which has given guidance on vocations for two thousand years is the gospel. That explains its place in this work, and I trust my readers will forgive me in advance when I ask for a certain familiarity with the sacred text.

II
Samuel, Samuel

Thinking about the problem of vocation and the relationships between young people and adults I am at once reminded of two famous people, Antigone and Samuel. Both of them on the threshold of adult life are faced with great responsibilities which they only partly understand, and which will lead them into great danger. But there the similarity ends. Whereas Samuel is guided in his first steps towards adult life by an experienced and understanding man, the tragic heroine Antigone has to work out her destiny alone with no guide but her conscience, and surrounded by people who, while professing to love her, are actually working to prevent her from doing what her conscience dictates. She might have had a happy life, secure in her position of power and privilege, but only if she had denied her true self, and given in to her fears, and refused to grow up. But there was something in this slip of a girl that gave her strength to defy the whole world, no matter what it might cost her. So a victim of power-politics became the symbol of the strength of the individual conscience in the struggle against tyranny.

What about Samuel, that attractive character from the

Bible? This, briefly, is his story. His mother had given him into the care of Eli, the High Priest, when he was barely weaned. Eli had incurred God's displeasure because he had allowed his sons to profit by their father's high status and to grow rich at the expense of those who came to worship and pray in the temple. Because God disapproved he was no longer talking to Eli, who must have been very upset as a result, for as High Priest he was considered to be God's spokesman, and to be the spokesman of a God who said nothing must have been mortifying indeed.

Young Samuel lived with Eli in the Temple. One night God called to him, 'Samuel, Samuel!' Now Samuel had never before heard the voice of God, and thinking his master needed him, ran to Eli and said, 'Here I am, what do you want?' But Eli sent him back saying he must have been dreaming. Samuel went to lie down again, but a moment later God called again, 'Samuel, Samuel!' The lad returned to the old man but he again sent him back to bed. When Samuel presented himself a third time to Eli, thinking he had been called, Eli at last took the boy's story seriously. Perceiving that God had called him he said, 'It is not I that called you, but God. Go back to bed and if God calls you again, say, "Speak, your servant is listening." '

God had much to say to Samuel that night, things that he would have preferred not to hear. He told him that he was going to punish Eli for being unfaithful to his priestly vocation. The next morning Eli, who suspected that the message was meant for him, asked Samuel to repeat everything he had been told. Then, humbly acknowledging that God was right to be displeased, Eli repented.

Here then was an experienced man who, though unfaithful

to his own calling, was able to show a very young man how to listen to God, whom he himself had not heard speaking for a long time. And in setting out to follow God's way, this boy whom God had chosen needed the help of an adult, even one who had gone astray, one who had ceased to follow God's way himself. This interdependence of the generations strikes me as something beautiful. Even though the adult may feel he has nothing more to say to the young person, it is still his duty to guide him towards adult life, and particularly into a relationship with God, to show him how to distinguish between the voice of God and that of human beings, and how to respond. This is the duty of each generation towards the one coming after it, irrespective of personal holiness. We are never unworthy to show the way of God to a young person, even when we have to say with more or less humility, 'Do as I say and not as I do.' And if the adult has fulfilled his responsibility he may be rewarded by hearing from the mouth of the young person that word which God could not speak to him directly because his ears were no longer able to hear it.

III
Musical Vocation

The great Belgian baritone José Vandam relates that at the age of twelve he knew without a shadow of doubt that he would be a singer. Yet his voice was breaking and he might have lost it, in which case singing would be out of the question. Against all the evidence he never doubted his vocation. Was his family such a musical one that the atmosphere at home encouraged, or even propelled him in that direction? Not at all. His family boasted not one musician and had no special connections, and yet his parents recognized his vocation and encouraged it. His music teacher, who thought the boy had a voice of some promise, got in touch with a famous singing-master. 'I have here a young boy whose voice is beginning to break. They are making him sing too much in the parish choir. If something isn't done soon his voice will be ruined.'

The singing-master arranged to meet the boy together with his parents, his teacher and the parish priest. Listening to young José, he knew that although the voice now sounded terrible because it was in the middle of breaking, there were signs, discernible only to himself, which gave promise of outstanding quality. So he told the priest not to make José sing any more because this would destroy his voice, and took him on as his pupil. Until his voice had completely broken he never made him sing during lessons, but sang himself instead. The teacher sang and the pupil had to correct him. The teacher would make mistakes on purpose, and such was the accuracy of the pupil's ear that he would quickly spot what was wrong. And so it was that José Vandam learnt to sing without singing himself, and embarked on a distinguished career as an opera singer.

This may serve as a parable of the relationship between adults and young people when a vocation is emerging, when the young person knows in their heart of hearts what they want to be. Many obstacles must be overcome, including risks springing from the vocation itself: to sing while the voice was breaking was the greatest danger for the future singer. Don Bosco dealt in the same way with Dominic Savio when he realized that the boy, in his desire for perfection, was undertaking fasts and penances which, during the period of his rapid growth to maturity, might damage his health, and in the long term might work against his vocation.

The need at this stage is for perceptive adults, unprejudiced parents, and someone with the special skill to discern the essential ingredients of a genuine vocation. The task of these specialists is to give whatever they can from their own experience to young people, not in order to teach them anything, but in order that they may confirm what their vocation has already told them, and what they already know in their heart to be true.

Only the master can discern the adult, with the adult's individual gifts and talents, already within the child, and it is the master's vocation to bring that adult to birth.

IV
The Secular Vocation

Parents need to be reminded that there really is such a thing as a secular vocation. When adults ask the child or adolescent their penetrating question, 'What are you going to be when you grow up?' the reply they get is sometimes surprising, even baffling, and all too often they receive it sceptically. The reply that they want to be like papa is so much easier to deal with. And there is nothing wrong with that! Like the gravedigger's son who without any trace of irony answered that when he grew up he would be a gravedigger like papa. There is no such thing as a silly trade or profession! But when a child is attracted towards a different kind of life, an occupation never followed by any other member of the family, or even something that has never been done before, it is then that he or she has most need of understanding and encouragement. The pioneer along any particular route always has the hardest journey.

Of course some childish ambitions make no more sense than dreams. But if our childhood dreams are taken seriously we are helped towards the moment of awakening when we shall be able to make our own realistic assessment of our hopes for the future. Mockery and misunderstanding will only cause us to withdraw into our imagination, where the dream takes on the appearance of reality. From this fantasy we shall find it harder and harder to tear ourselves away, and the awakening, when it comes at last, will be all the more cruel and harmful. As children we need freedom to explore our own personalities. Let the adults, together with us, marvel at the gifts and talents which gradually come to light, one after another. The day will come when our true vocation will become clear within our heart and mind, and that is when we shall need to know that we can trust the adults completely. The only people able to give us the support we need then will be those who did not smile at our childhood dreams, but, by accepting us as we were, helped us to find out exactly what the dreams meant.

As young people thinking about our future, we are trying to know and understand ourselves better, and we deserve to be respected and taken seriously. Even when our speech is still childish, even when the image we have of ourselves is still influenced in all kinds of ways of which we cannot yet be fully aware, our elders have absolutely no right to laugh at our plans, our ambitions and dreams, indeed, in so doing they might even be murdering a Mozart or a Pasteur.

Vocations in the secular sense are a fact of life, and everybody has one, because we are all called to realize our personality to the full. Those who grasp this truth in good time are lucky indeed; the knowledge will give them the strength and persistence to undergo rigorous physical or intellectual discipline and to use every opportunity to develop their potential abilities. Think, for instance, of the strict dieting and the physical and mental effort necessary for the training of a top-level athlete, or the grinding toil and untiring perseverance required for the mastery of a musical instrument. We have only to consider the feats of ingenuity, skill, courage, endurance and concentration, and the strength of character displayed by so many young people in pursuit of their goals, to be convinced that there is a source of strength nourishing them, and a self-awareness supporting them and carrying them along.

How fortunate they are! But how unfortunate those who, since their infancy, have not been treated as persons in their own right; who have not been encouraged to believe in themselves, to discover themselves, or to wish to make something of themselves. Their personalities will be stunted indefinitely, like pollarded trees which, unable to grow normally, become grossly misshapen and look like nothing on earth. People who have failed to fulfil their personalities use their talents and energy in the same disorderly manner. They may even reach positions of prestige, but in the depths of their hearts they are bitter at having wasted their life by not really being themselves.

Unfortunately the harm does not stop there. These wounded personalities project their frustrated hopes on to their children, becoming ambitious on their behalf, seeking to realize vicariously the achievements of which they themselves were not capable. The resulting complication and tension is unbearable, because they are seeking not their children's happiness, but their own by proxy. Hence the spectacle of unfortunate children crushed by the weight of a responsibility which is not really theirs. They are compelled to become what their parents want them to be, and are imprisoned in a happiness that was not designed for them. All their lives they will have the sensation of struggling under a burden too heavy for them to bear, or of wearing a suit of clothes made for someone bigger.

I know some parents who believed that leaving money to their children would have had the effect of handicapping them for life. Instead, they have had given them every opportunity to use whatever talents they possessed. They have imbued them with the desire to learn, and have encouraged them to aim for the highest standards. They have loyally supported them in their schemes. All this they have done to the best of their ability so that their children might grow into adults capable of making adult choices and carrying them through to completion. But it was always understood that nothing further was to be expected, and that, free from the burden of being sons and daughters of papa, their happiness and fulfilment would be entirely of their own making.

The result is that in this family an astonishing variety of personalities have been free to develop. One daughter has made her career in singing, another in the theatre. One son, with such a craze for space travel that he had organized a club, and made rockets and launched them, now works in an observatory. Another is a journalist like his father. Whilst the mother, suddenly widowed, has successfully embarked on a career in politics.

V

The Individual Person

Biology teaches us something that we knew already, but it needs underlining: that no two human beings are alike. Each human being is unique from the moment of conception because his or her genetic code is different from all those who have ever existed or ever will exist.

If all individuals are different from the very beginning, every human being must be strictly unique and irreplaceable, possessing an assortment of human characteristics which that person alone can develop, for only that individual has the key, or, if we may apply to a living being a term borrowed from information technology, only that individual has the programme.

This biological truth – that all human beings are different and each individual is unique – ought to make us think about the responsibility which parents and society have. We owe it to a unique and irreplaceable being to allow it to develop as fully as it can so that whatever is new or original about it can be added to the inheritance of the human race. The rest of the personality, all that it has in common with other people, whilst still entitled to respect, is not exactly irreplaceable.

21

Accordingly it is in the interest of both the individual and society that what differentiates one from all the others should be discovered and developed as fully as possible. I wouldn't be so cruel as to dwell on modern methods of education and upbringing in the light of this principle, since it is all too obvious that the virtues they prize most are conformity and uniformity. We are successful, even very successful, in developing the traits that we have in common, but we do it at the cost of obliterating our differences. We have a certain method of production that takes no account of the happiness of the workers. In human terms the cost of such a system is very high. Whereas, for all we know, an alternative method, designed with the workers' happiness in mind, would be no less efficient, with the bonus that they would bring infinitely more creativity to their work.

But no matter how society is organized there will always be exceptional people who do not fit in, people of strong character, who refuse to become slaves of convention, and choose rather to fulfil their own personalities. These people are likely to be marginalized. There are the luxury class of the marginalized — those who have succeeded in making themselves indispensable — who are lionized, fêted and heaped with honours and riches; and there are the really marginalized — those whom nobody needs — who are the objects of pity, scorn or condemnation. But whether you are pushed aside by 'normal' people, or pushed up above out of their reach, it comes to the same thing.

A person is not just made up of matter, even matter endowed with intelligence. Our faith tells us that at the moment of conception, when two persons become one flesh through the love they have for each other, to the extent that a new life comes into being which is both the continuation and the transformation of their two lives – at that moment God intervenes in a creative act. This is a fascinating and delightful mystery, which I cannot begin to explain. God loves every human being with a creative love that makes him or her a person.

I cannot imagine God reaching the limit of his inventiveness and having to create the same thing twice. God does not repeat himself. He is truly a creator and he is never short of new ideas. This means that if everyone is already biologically different, *a fortiori* the personal love of God for each individual makes him or her unique in other ways. Let us suppose that two persons had exactly the same genetic code, and that the upbringing of these perfect twins had been in every respect identical; their personalities would still not be replicas of each other, because the personal love with which God loved each one would still be unique.

If a mother is able to recognize her twins, who look exactly alike to strangers, and to love each in a different way, how much more does God see us as distinct and essentially different.

It is here, therefore, that we might expect to find the true root of the personality, its essential individuality and uniqueness. Perhaps that is why it could be said, 'Only God is human.' It is a mysterious fact that a person is most truly human at the point where he or she encounters God.

VI
Words of the Word

God loves all people, but he does not love them *en masse*. He loves each one personally. God loves me just as I am. He always has loved me and always will. His love for me is constant. He believes in me. He loves you just as you are. He always has loved you and always will. His love for you is constant. He believes in you. God loves that person . . . He knows us better than we know ourselves. St Augustine assures us that he is closer to us than we are to ourselves. He knows us so well because he created us.

At the moment that the mutual love between our parents brought about our conception, God loved us as persons and gave us life, or, as we might say, he pronounced a word of life. At the moment that the chromosomes from our parents united to form the particular programme which would develop throughout our growing period to produce a human being different from all others – with the mother's eyes, the father's hair, a particular character and level of intelligence, a propensity to this or that illness, a certain blood group . . . all these characteristics inherited from our parents, obeying laws at once precise and so complex that no two human beings are exactly alike –

at that moment God called us by our name, a new name never before pronounced or heard. The word was a creative one and, as with every word from God, was not spoken in vain.

This mysterious name distinguishes us one from another more completely than any of our other characteristics. This word uttered once and for all states who we truly are: we are words of the Word. The essential distinction between persons is the supernatural one, the word of God spoken at our conception. The kiss of the Eternal within time, imparting his image, his icon.

It is up to us to make this image visible in our humanity, after the example of Jesus, the Word, who has spoken to us in human language. The Word was expressed fully in human words, gestures, actions and feelings. So too the word of God spoken at our conception must be expressed in our humanity. That is our responsibility alone, and only thus shall we be fulfilled as persons. Our natural self (that which our parents conceived in their love) can find fulfilment, but that is like the clay model fashioned by God in the story of creation, before God had breathed life into it. We too need God's life-giving breath, calling us to a super-natural life, to the fulfilment of our spiritual self. We are to use our life to proclaim openly that word of God which we are, and to make it intelligible, so that it may not remain a dead letter or disappear without an echo into the silence of death or nothingness. This is our astonishing privilege: to incarnate a word of God. And for this purpose we are indispensable and irreplaceable, because no other person can be that word of God in our stead. By being that word we are a unique gift for all humankind.

To be human, therefore, consists in discovering what word God spoke when he created us, and acting in such a way that this word is translated into 'human speech' by means of our life. To be human means to recognize who we are, to take responsibility for ourselves, to accept ourselves as we are. Not to force ourselves artificially into a copy of someone else, but letting ourselves develop in our own way.

God reveals us to ourselves. He gives us the courage to accept what we are and the strength to become what we ought to be. Very often our vocation is something which we do not want, but which we have to acknowledge is right for us, if only we are honest with ourselves. It is God who calls us by our true name, the one known to him and ourselves alone, and which indicates for us the way to true happiness.

VII
Who Are We?

When we reach the age of making decisions that will determine the direction of our adult life, the most important question facing us is: Who are we really, and what is the word that God wants to speak in us and through us?

How can we know who we are? Since we are a word of God, we shall know who we are by listening to God's voice speaking in us. If we do not hear it, the odds are not that it has fallen silent, but rather that we are hard of hearing. God is speaking to us, of that we may be certain, and our part is to be silent and listen. We are like transistor radios crackling and buzzing, and we must adjust ourselves to God's wavelength. He is transmitting twenty four hours a day nonstop, and all we have to do is tune in to him. Many other voices within us are causing interference and we must learn to recognize the voice of our conscience, to discern its tone amidst the confused noise of our desires and urges, and all the other pressures exerted upon us, both internal and external.

The voice of conscience can be muffled, but we may be sure that we shall always be able to recognize it amongst all the other voices, provided only that we are sufficiently attentive. Conscience is the bearer of God's word. It is like the curvature of the soul under the influence of the gravitational field of an infinite force. Made up as we are of reasonableness and common sense, conscience opens us up to another dimension. It is the point at which the continuum of life and matter breaks down in order to allow the existence of free human persons. It is where we discover ourselves as distinct from others, able to exercise our free will, persons in our own right. Here, in the depths of our self-awareness, we can hear a voice, not that of our conscience, but one which enables the conscience to be heard: and this is the voice of God. At this level we have the strongest sensation of existing, because we find out that at least we exist for someone, and that someone is God. It is God who is our true partner in dialogue, who will never let us down, who alone sees into our inmost hearts; who, far from wanting to change us into something different, will help us to become what we really are.

Knowing that God is present and to be encountered among those who love one another, we seem to hear the inner voice amplified as if by a loudspeaker, and to sense our own existence even more strongly. God, our creator and partner in dialogue, displays a human face. It is Jesus in the other person. But the other person must be silence personified, that is, Mary.

VIII
The Calling of Jesus

How did Jesus become aware of his own vocation? We can see him beginning to understand even while he was still a child; the gospel is quite explicit about it. You will remember the strange story: how Jesus stayed behind in the Temple at the age of twelve. Thinking they had lost him, his parents searched amongst the other pilgrims for three days, and then in Jerusalem. And they were astonished to find him at last among the theologians and clergy, quite unabashed by these dignitaries, listening to them and asking them questions, impressing them all with his intelligence. 'How could you do this?' said his mother. 'You've given us the fright of our lives.' 'Why were you looking for me?' he replied. 'Didn't you know that I must be about my Father's business?' But they were baffled by this. Then he returned home with them and was subject to them.

He was scarcely more than a child, yet he knew he must be about his Father's business, and that his Father was God. This awareness must have been pretty strong for a good child to behave so strangely. Jesus knew that he was called to his Father's business. But his parents did not understand and Jesus returned home with them and was subject to them. That shows clearly that children can have such an understanding with God that they know that God is calling them to attend to his business. But the people around do not understand. If Mary and Joseph did not understand Jesus on that occasion, it is safe to bet that other parents do not understand their children. So we should not let it worry us, it is normal.

Parents do not understand because they fail to see what is happening to their children: they are starting to become adults. They are always seen as children because they still look like children and have childish needs. Jesus recognized and understood these limitations without difficulty: he returned home and was subject to them. A long time was to elapse before what he announced at the age of twelve would come to be put into practice. When his hour came, then his vocation would be fulfilled.

I believe that many young people have had similar thoughts during their childhood or adolescence, but their ideas of their Father's business and how to be busy with it turn out to be very different from what they actually do as adults. They develop physically and psychologically, emotionally and intellectually, and when they are grown up they behave differently from when they were children, even though they are aware of an essential continuity.

IX

The Calling of the Disciples

It is strange but true that Jesus was unable to carry out his Father's plans all by himself; it was his will to need helpers. In theory there seems no reason why he should not have acted alone. He was, after all, the Son of God. As the Word of God he could easily have changed the world. But he did not do it that way precisely because he was human, limited in space and time. His life would be of a certain duration, tied to a certain place. He would meet a certain number of people and no more. Being unable all by himself to carry out his Father's plans, he would call men and women to co-operate with him in fulfilling his mission.

How did the first disciples of Jesus come to join him? Curiously enough, it is in the account of Jesus' baptism that we learn about the calling of the first two disciples, John (the future evangelist) and his friend Andrew. To judge from what we can learn of John's psychology, he was still very young at the time, but he had already made a serious commitment, for like Andrew he was a disciple of John the Baptist. After the baptism John the Baptist pointed Jesus out to them with the words, 'That is the Lamb of God.'

By then Jesus had already departed, following the bank

of the Jordan, but John and Andrew set out after him, literally following in his footsteps.

Undoubtedly they were a little anxious, and did not know quite how to behave. Not being bold enough to accost Jesus directly they walked behind him at a respectful distance. We can picture Jesus varying his pace to make sure that they were following him on purpose. In any case it was Jesus who took the initiative. Turning round he asked what they wanted. They were taken by surprise and replied (as they were to do so often afterwards!) with the first piece of nonsense that came to mind, 'We want to see where you are living.' 'Very well,' Jesus replied, 'come home with me.' And they spent two days at his house.

This story teaches us several useful lessons. First of all, we notice that Jesus is brought to the young men's attention by John the Baptist. This shows the importance of a friend ready to give disinterested advice. John the Baptist encouraged them to detach themselves from him and follow their own vocation, even though he knew he would lose two of his disciples in the process.

Secondly, there is the sheer simplicity of these young men who, without knowing exactly where they were going, or even realizing quite what they were doing, set off to follow Jesus. Action preceded reflection on their part. I believe that, just as very young people perceive their vocation in a typically childish way, they also have a characteristic way of responding to Jesus, which tends to be romantic, even exaggerated. They don't know where they are going, they just go, and that is the important thing. What strikes us is that from that moment onwards Jesus takes charge. He stops, turns round and speaks to them. He shows no irritation at their reply which, taken literally, makes little sense. The young men say they want to see where he lives, so he takes them there. He really shares their interests, and listens to what they say. He does not judge them, but accepts them as they are. But Jesus's true home is his eternal one, his divine sonship. In taking the two friends to 'his home' he indeed gives them what they ask, but in a way that far exceeds their expectations. Bowled over by this experience they go to find Peter, saying, 'Come and see. We think we have found the Messiah.' Peter is simple-hearted, despite his greater maturity, and listens willingly to what Jesus has to say.

Then they all go together to look for Nathanael, a thoughtful man, and deeply spiritual. The news that the Messiah has been found, and that it is Jesus from Nazareth, is hard for Nathanael to swallow. His response, 'Can anything good come out of Nazareth?' shows his religious training, perhaps combined with a rather small-town mentality. His sceptical nature will not allow him to be carried away by any kind of enthusiasm. He must be presented with incontrovertible facts. Jesus treats him as he needs to be treated. Since he needs a fact, he will get it. 'By the way,' Jesus says, apparently casually, 'I saw you just now under the fig tree.' What actually happened at that moment the gospel does not tell us. But, in acknowledging this fact, Nathanael understands that Jesus has observed him and has seen him for what he really is.

Previously Jesus had told him that he was a true Israelite, with nothing false about him. This was remarkable coming from Jesus, whom Nathanael had just indirectly insulted with his less than flattering opinion of his native village. But Jesus justifies him by saying that there is nothing false in him, a response that surprises Nathanael. He knows himself to be honest and without falseness, but wonders how Jesus could have divined this, since they have only just met, and Jesus has had nothing from him but discourtesy.

So Jesus becomes more specific: he tells him that he has seen him under the fig tree. Nathanael realizes that Jesus has been interested in him for some time past, as a person. Judging by Nathanael's reply, we gather that the moment when Jesus noticed him under the fig tree must have been for him a moment of crucial importance, or of revelation, a turning-point in his life, since he replies, 'Rabbi, you are the Son of God, you are the King of Israel.' In other words, 'You could not have known that if you were an ordinary man.'

Because he feels that he is known and loved to the very depths of his being, he has an insight into the personality of Jesus. So he joins the group of Jesus' companions. And we see how his religious background, after first acting as a brake, now enables him, once his reservations are overcome, to make a commitment that is all the stronger for being tried and tested.

X

The Marriage at Cana

Accompanied by a group of his disciples Jesus had begun to preach publicly. One day he was invited to a wedding, together with his mother and his companions. Once again we see Jesus living an ordinary human life, accepting the conventions and obligations of society, and celebrating family festivals with his friends and relations. You will remember that at a certain moment the wine ran out. Seeing what had happened, Mary said to Jesus, 'They have no more wine.' Her intuition told her that although Jesus had never worked a miracle before, it was in his power to save the newly married couple from embarrassment.

Jesus, however, seems not to agree. 'What business is it of yours?' he says. 'My hour has not yet come.' His hour, that is the whole point. The hour, in other words, of his vocation; the moment fixed by the Father, when he will be called to a direct involvement in his Father's business. The misunderstanding he had with Mary when he was twelve, and had been lost, now seems to be repeated. But this time Mary apparently understands the nature of her son's vocation before he does, realizing that D-day has come.

Mary presses him no further, but advises the servants

to do whatever Jesus tells them. And, as often in the gospels, Jesus is persuaded to work a miracle by the ready co-operation of people who are not themselves particularly religious. This is the first sign he performs, and because of it his disciples believe in him.

So this is a very important day for the first disciples. Here is the proof they were waiting for. Now they can believe in Jesus unreservedly. The astonishing thing is that the background to this crucial event is not the overpowering grandeur and symbolism of a storm at sea, or the cloud on Tabor, but the hubbub and joyful commotion of a wedding, where the wine flows like water.

XI
Fishers of Men

At the marriage in Cana the disciples began to believe in Jesus and to feel his influence more strongly, but they were not yet wholly set apart to follow him. Their lives went on much as usual. They were still living at home, diligently earning their daily bread by their various trades. Jesus had not yet taken to the roads with them. There were yet several stages which they must pass through before reaching maturity as disciples.

One day Jesus was on the shore of Lake Gennesaret, hemmed in by a crowd of people who were listening to him, and he noticed two boats moored to the bank. The fishermen had disembarked and were washing their nets. He climbed into one of the boats, belonging to Simon, and asked him to pull out a little way from the shore; then he sat down and taught the crowd from the boat. Afterwards he said to Simon, 'Move out into deep water and let down your nets for a catch.' Simon replied, 'Master, we have toiled all night long and have caught nothing. Nevertheless, at your word I will let down the nets.' When they had done this they caught such a large quantity of fish that their nets were breaking. So they signalled to their friends in the other boat to come and help them. Working together, they filled both boats so full that they were beginning to capsize. When he saw this Simon Peter fell to his knees saying, 'Depart from me, for I am a sinful man.' He and his companions were stupefied by the catch that they had made. So too were James and John, the sons of Zebedee, Simon's partners. But Jesus said to Simon, 'Don't be afraid, from now on you are going to catch people.' Then, when they had brought their boats to shore, they left everything and followed him.

Jesus had been preparing to call Peter, James and John to follow him, but before bringing them to the point of decision he first caused them to experience something extra-ordinary, the miraculous catch of fish. After an exhausting and fruitless night's work they had returned empty-handed under the mocking gaze of the little crowd who were gathered to hear Jesus. Worn out and dejected, they had washed their nets without saying a word. It was then that Jesus told Peter to try again for a catch. Peter, who knew his trade perfectly well, replied, 'If we have laboured all night without success, we are not likely to catch anything now, in broad daylight, with dry nets. But if it gives you any pleasure . . . ' And so occurred the most extraordinary episode in Peter's experience as a fisherman, a catch beyond his wildest dreams.

It is not Jesus' way to take advantage of our times of failure in order to call us, as if to say, 'Now that you have messed up your life, you might as well go into a seminary.' On the contrary, he demonstrates to Peter that with his help he can achieve exceptional success in the way of life he is actually engaged in. Then, at the moment when Peter is experiencing perfect fulfilment as a fisherman and as a human being, Jesus reveals that he has something more to offer, something still greater to achieve: to become a fisher of people.

But such a vivid encounter with God causes Peter to take fright: 'Depart from me, for I am a sinner.' Peter, certainly, is unworthy to draw near to the Son of God incarnate, but who would be worthy? At the moment when we decide to follow Jesus a temptation springs up, a deadly scruple poisoning the heart. It says, 'I am not worthy; I am not brave enough; I am not strong enough.' At the very moment when Jesus comes near, intending to share his life with us, we ask him to keep away. Our misplaced humility, which is really more akin to pride, forbids him entrance to our heart. But Jesus then says to us what he said to Peter, when he was fearful because of the terrible strangeness of what he had seen: 'Don't be anxious, don't be afraid!' And he restores our peace of mind, without which we should be unable to follow him.

XII
No One is Safe

Peter, although a fundamentally good man, honest and hardworking, was in his own estimation a sinner. But there was a class of people who were dubbed sinners by public opinion, with whom all contact was forbidden. Merely to shake hands with one of them, or to visit their houses or eat at their table was a breach of the Jewish law. Such were the tax-collectors hired by the Romans to collect customs duties. In a society living under Roman occupation they were hated as collaborators who shamelessly lined their pockets at the expense of their fellow citizens.

Clearly, if there was one person who could feel immune from any call by Jesus it was the Levi, the tax-collector. Protected by his reputation as a notorious public sinner, he could relax in the knowledge that he was perfectly safe. Jesus, being a man of God, would not be able even to speak to him. But the gospel tells us, 'Afterwards he went out, and saw a tax-collector, named Levi, sitting at his customs post, and said to him, "Follow me." And he left everything, and rose and followed him.' That says it all. Truly no one is safe!

Just when we think we are beyond the reach of any divine call because of our particular circumstances, Bang! – the call is targeted precisely on us. And why is this? Jesus explains that he has come not for the righteous and the healthy, but for the sake of sinners and the sick. He is not worried about our hang-ups, or other people's bad opinion of us, even if it is well-founded. He prejudges no one. There is nothing to stop him from coming to us whenever he likes with the invitation to follow him.

XIII
Who Chooses Whom?

When the disciples began to follow Jesus it was not because he had called them. After his baptism, when those first two followed him along the bank of the Jordan, Jesus asked what they wanted and allowed them to go with him to his house, and they stayed there for two days before going home to tell their families and neighbours all about it. So news about Jesus spread, and other people began to join the little group surrounding him. Jesus let them come, and even invited them to accompany him to the wedding where he was to be a guest, and there they witnessed the miracle that convinced them that he was the Messiah. But although they were going about with Jesus, they continued to live at their own homes and to earn their living as they usually did.

Then there came a more explicit call to follow Jesus, and they left everything to follow him on his tour of Palestine. But it was not until much later that Jesus chose a certain number of them to be his apostles, in other words called them to a real vocation. For this momentous occasion he prepared himself by spending a night in prayer on the mountain. First, then, Jesus grants us the desire to become his disciples, and only later, choosing the moment with great care, does he reveal the task he wants to entrust to us. The first disciples were free to come and go as they chose, but they stayed loyally with Jesus, although he asked nothing of them. He was waiting for them to mature. When he felt that they could be treated seriously as adults, he began to tell them about his Father's business, speaking to them as equals. Then he prayed to the Father to find out his plan for them, and revealed it to them.

Those who attached themselves to Jesus did so of their own free will; indeed, they were exercising a freedom that they had learnt in the course of their friendship with him. They could have resumed their independent life at any time, and lived it in accordance with Jesus' will, but they chose rather to throw in their lot completely with him, to follow him without looking back or counting the cost. And the cost, as Jesus quite openly taught them, would be high. After the feeding of the five thousand, when the crowds heard Jesus' stern teaching about the bread of life and began to drift away, Jesus also gave his friends another chance to leave him, but they chose to stay, replying, 'To whom should we go? You alone have the words of life.' At the end of his life, however, Jesus would open his heart to them and show them the truth: 'You did not choose me, but I chose you.'

The apostles could legitimately believe that they had chosen Jesus, because they had left everything in order to follow him, whereas Jesus had asked nothing of them. Indeed, not only had he made no attempt to attract them by promises of fame, riches or power, but he had done all that he could to put them off by emphasizing their duty to take up their cross daily, and to put their families, their work, and themselves in second place. The apostles had been conscious of acting with complete freedom when they followed Jesus, but the truth was that Jesus had already loved them and chosen them.

XIV

Looking on him, he loved him

Everyone whom Jesus called, he loved personally and individually. We read in the gospel about an occasion of a disappointment for Jesus, when he called a rich young man. What happened shows beyond a doubt that Jesus never brought pressure on any one to follow him. The young man, a model of virtue, and filled with zeal to do good, comes to Jesus and says, 'Good master, what must I do to inherit eternal life?' The reply is not: 'That's easy. All you have to do is come with me.' On the contrary, Jesus reminds him of the key principles which govern his religious life as a Jewish believer.

This answer does not satisfy him. 'All these I have observed from my youth. What do I still lack?' The gospel then notes, touchingly, 'Jesus, looking on him, loved him.' Jesus has done everything he could to avoid making this young man face up to the harsh demands of his vocation. He is so full of good intentions; how useful he would be when the harvest is so abundant and labourers so few! He could be recruited straightaway. But no, Jesus gives the mildest possible reply. He has a vocation of his own, and is scrupulously faithful to it. Not even for

45

the best of causes will he use psychological or religious pressure to attract his followers.

It is almost as if he is so aware of the dangers which lie in wait for the disciple that he tries to deter him. One must be willing to die for the sake of the kingdom of heaven. But the young man will not be put off and Jesus is forced to say more. Moved by the evident sincerity of the young man's desire for perfection, he looks at him with love and deep understanding. The young man has challenged God, and now God gives his answer, turning on him the full strength and fierceness of his love: 'If you want to be perfect, go, sell all that you have and give it to the poor, and then follow me.'

It is hard to know for certain what our vocation is, because although we may consider that we are in a fit state to hear what God intends for us, he is reluctant to speak. We must, as it were, force his hand and make him call us; we have to wrest from Jesus that loving attention which he bestowed on the young man before he called him to follow him.

The rich young man gave up the idea of following Jesus, because he had great possessions, but other people who have experienced the same personal love of Jesus for them have gone on to hear him say, in the end, 'You did not choose me, but I chose you.' What a wonderful glimpse into the heart of God! For God every person is intrinsically precious. That we should choose God is not particularly surprising, but that he should choose us is quite extraordinary. How can we possibly matter to him as much as that?

XV

The Moment of Choice

The time comes when we realize that our freedom comes from God, and that he intends us to exercise it. This knowledge is a source of strength, enabling us to choose confidently from among the various inclinations within us that one which corresponds most closely to our true self, weighing it against other possibilities which we also find attractive. So we may see clearly that we ought to follow our inclination for marriage, instead of some other way of life to which we are also attracted. Or we may decide to enter a religious community, despite being attracted to marriage; or to become a priest, unless we are drawn to one of the other forms of consecrated life that exist today, such as the Focolare. But until we are aware of this total freedom, and can see clearly what we want, it is important to make no final decision, to do nothing that is irreversible.

This does not mean that we should have no idea about what we shall decide in the end. It is quite possible to know a long time in advance that we shall one day follow a certain vocation, without finally committing ourselves, because the right moment has not yet come. Then it comes. It is like being in love, then engaged, then making active preparations for the wedding. All this might take several years. Then comes the moment when we exchange our vows and become, from that time onwards, man and wife.

That is the moment of decision, when the irrevocable commitment is made. I believe strongly that if we have already committed ourselves before the marriage, we have made a grave mistake.

'Living together' sounds harmless enough, but the discreetness of the language is thoroughly misleading, concealing as it does the dangerous commitments being made too early. You cannot say yes to a sexual relationship without involving yourself and your partner in a commitment, whether you are aware of it or not. Nor is it possible to live together, to share bed and board with someone, without creating some sort of common ownership of property, and that involves another commitment that is mutual, personal and public.

We ought not to bind ourselves like this until we have made a final choice, otherwise we empty our commitment of its meaning. Every vocation needs to unfold, step by step. If we take these steps before making a proper decision, we tie ourselves down prematurely, and never experience that freedom which gives us the power to be faithful to our commitments.

The only way that I can see to be sure of making the right choice and staying faithful to it for the rest of our life is to trust completely in God's love and in his intentions for us, practising a certain detachment from immediate concerns. As we shall then discover, true happiness does not come from selfishly grabbing what we want from life. It is the gift of God.

Moreover, this willingness to postpone final decisions, to trust completely in God's love for us, does not necessarily exclude our original plans. They might still be fulfilled in the end, but if we wait we can come to know for certain that what happens to us will be according to God's plan, and will result in the unfolding of our true personality.

Then we shall be sure that the person we marry is the one whom we can make happy, and who can make us happy.

This necessary self-restraint, this period of engagement, matters just as much for the future priest or nun. If we become a priest, we want to know for certain that in the priesthood lies our best chance of being happy and of making others happy. If we join a religious community we should have no doubt that our real spiritual family is here, and that in this family our capacity for giving and receiving love can be best expressed, for our own happiness and for the good of the Church.

XVI
Marriage or Celibacy?

E ven to talk about a choice between marriage and celibacy, a decision which will have a fundamental effect on our life, shows that we have enough confidence in God's love to believe that such a thing as celibacy is possible. Otherwise, why should we ever ask the question, since it simply would not apply to us? Probably it would not arise at all, unless someone put it into our minds, which rarely happens these days in the way that it used to. There can be few parents or teachers who think of celibacy otherwise than as a form of mutilation or incapacity. They could even, if they wanted to, express their disapproval in words borrowed from Jesus himself, who said emphatically that there is no earthly reason for not getting married, meaning, no good human reason.

Jesus puts it so harshly that translations have tended to soften his words. The subject came up during a discussion of the question: if a man is tired of his wife, under what conditions can he get rid of her? According to Jewish law, provided the husband certified in writing that he had taken the initiative and was sending her away, all was in order. There was no need for the woman actually to have left home. Jesus, whilst he acknowledges that the law was designed to prevent yet graver abuses, challenges it as falling short of God's original plan. And he goes on to speak of marriage in a way which his hearers find revolutionary, calling it a divine institution, created by God. 'Those whom God has joined together, let no man put asunder.' At this point the apostles exclaim, 'In that case, it is better not to marry.'

So the question does arise, and it is not a frivolous one. The disciples, newly aware of the true nature of marriage and its importance in God's eyes, ask whether it is really possible. Jesus replies somewhat obliquely. There are eunuchs, he explains, people who cannot marry because they are by nature incomplete, lacking genital organs, for instance, or otherwise physically or psychologically unsuited for marriage. Others are made eunuchs by other people, either literally castrated, as was the practice at that time, or prevented from marrying by social considerations, such as too great a disparity in social standing. But there are also eunuchs who have become so for the sake of the kingdom of heaven. And he adds, 'Only those who have been called can understand this.'

Elsewhere in the gospel Jesus, returning to the same question, says that there is no reason on earth not to marry, and that the motive can only be heavenly. So normally the question of celibacy does not arise. There might be people who for whatever reason, of health or character, judge that in marriage they will not be happy, and decide not to marry. God will not abandon them and is able to help them to make something positive of their life, but this does not mean that their 'choice' has anything at all to do with a vocation to celibacy. The same applies to those who for family reasons, social convenience, the intervention of war, or any other outside cause, find it impossible to marry. None of this has anything to do with vocation. It is not God who is leading them to stay unmarried. He shares their suffering and comforts them, but he has had no part in their choice. Excepting these two classes of people there is, according to Jesus, no human motive for thinking of anything other than following our strong natural inclination towards marriage.

To be frank, I wonder whether marriage as a form of commitment is all that 'natural'. Current practice among young people today suggests that it is not. We need to distinguish properly between the active expression of our sexuality, to which we are constantly urged by nature, and true marriage, which is waiting to be rediscovered, or even reinvented.

The extraordinary thing is that the question of whether to stay unmarried still arises at all, and that there are people who have not only asked themselves the question but have answered it positively, and live, apparently happily, in an unmarried state which they have chosen without any compulsion from nature or other people. That is a fact beyond dispute. It is significant, incidentally, that this phenomenon is not confined to the Christian culture, but is also to be found in other religious cultures, above all in Buddhism, but also in Hinduism, and in certain parts of Islam, although there it is more exceptional and altogether less acceptable.

Jesus tells us that the reasons are not earthly, only heavenly. Not 'inhuman', since people who choose celibacy have no sense of being that. Nor do they feel 'unnatural', although nature urges them away from celibacy, not towards it. Their choice arises out of a process of reasoning which is human, certainly, but human at its best, and not only that, but more profound as well; so much more profound that it amounts to another kind of logic, which perhaps we may presume to call 'supernatural'.

In any case, if the answer to this question is bothering us, if it is in our mind at all, the alternative logic must have already begun to affect the way we think, and the call of the supernatural, or God, or paradise, is making itself heard. Already we are convinced that our happiness and personal fulfilment are bound up with God's love for us. We know by faith that it is so. Although we may be inexperienced, and not yet in that state of total liberty which we shall enjoy one day, we already know enough to be clear about the general direction in which we must look for the truth about ourselves and our future. We have no explicit proof, so we risk the alternative logic, that of the love of God for us, a logic whose scope far exceeds our own concerns, which all the evidence of nature urges us to pursue: our self-cultivation and the quest for personal happiness.

When we are sure that God loves us, we also know that it is from this certainty that true happiness comes. But when we are feeling depressed, and are doubting whether God loves us at all, the notion of abandoning ourselves to God's love begins to look terribly dangerous. The sheer effort of clinging to belief, whilst being torn apart by inner conflicts, must not be underrated. Even if we do not doubt the existence of God, we can easily doubt his love, and that amounts to the same thing in practice, since God is love. It is hard to remain steadfast at times like these, and we may be tempted to settle for the more limited kind of happiness that nature openly offers us. This may be the moment for a genuine and courageous act of faith.

Religious faith does not rest on a straightforward appeal to evidence, leading to general agreement, nor is it a mystical state that we can just slip into without effort. It is a mature act of our free will which, to be real, must allow of the possibility of doubt; and obviously, if we doubt God's existence we cannot act on his call. But equally, just because our faith changes in character as we grow up, moving from a childish faith, which is taught, emotional and largely unreflective, to a mature faith, which is free, intelligent and voluntary, we cannot dismiss the call as an illusion. I know from personal experience that even while we are doubting the existence of God we can feel called by him. Of course, we cannot take any action in response to his call unless we believe that he exists, so that is the first question we need to settle, before we take any other decisions. If we are trying to decide between celibacy and marriage, there is no point in using the logic of human nature, because according to human nature celibacy makes no sense at all, so we know in advance what the answer is going to be, one of the options being ruled out *a priori*. We must rather take divine logic as our starting-point. I see no other course.

From God's point of view, what are the possibilities? Is marriage ruled out? Do people who believe in the love of God fall automatically into the category of eunuchs for the sake of the kingdom of heaven? That is what many people believe; and they go on to deduce that married people are therefore second-class Christians. They therefore believe that those who do not feel called to celibacy must rest content with being the faithful sheep of the flock, leaving others, the truly called, to take charge, that is the clergy and religious, whom they regard as the backbone, the brains and the heart of the Church.

Despite all the efforts of, for instance, the Second Vatican Council to restore the proper dignity of the laity, most people still equate the Church with its ordained ministers. The effect of this confusion is disastrous, because by pretending to put a value on certain vocations, it devalues the very notion of Christian vocation itself and renders apathetic the great majority of Church members. It cannot be said too strongly that whilst God calls some to celibacy, he just as positively calls others to marriage. The difference is that those who are not interested in knowing what God in his love plans for them, and simply follow their natural instinct, marry, since there is no such thing as celibacy in the natural order. Marriage as a vocation is therefore more difficult to distinguish than celibacy, for whereas celibacy is either a vocation or an unnatural state of frustration, marriage, even a purely natural one, provided it is well lived, is a source of happiness and stability. Therefore those who marry without asking whether they are called to it have nothing to reproach themselves for. I believe, however, that those who are courageous enough to ask what their true vocation is, prepared even for it to turn out to be celibacy, will in due course experience a different kind of marriage which is truly Christian. For such a couple the sacrament will have its full meaning and effect because they will realize the presence of Jesus is at the centre of their love, and will receive each other as a gift from God.

Since marriage is a sign of the love between Christ and his

Church, thoughtful husbands and wives come to understand that their marriage is God's gift to the whole Church, and a state of life to which they are called on behalf of the whole Church. Their choice is not precariously dependent on youth or beauty, but is reaffirmed each day until the end of their life. All who wish to follow Jesus must take up their cross daily. The cross of married people is, in a nutshell, to be faithful to each other and to their children. And to compensate for this, there will be times when they will know the heavenly joy of meeting the risen Jesus in each other. The essence of Christian marriage is to be aware that in choosing our partner we are choosing someone who from now on will be Jesus to us, for better for worse, as we say, Jesus crucified and Jesus risen. No marriage is without troubles, but the way to deal with them is to take them up daily as part of our cross, following Jesus. Then we shall know the mysterious presence of God in our marriage and shall experience the joy of paradise.

So as I see it, God does call people to marriage, but to a particular marriage, not just to any marriage. Marriage of this kind is based on the logic of God, on our certainty that God loves us and our future spouse. Since God has made us for each other, he will inevitably bring us to meet each other if we let him, when we are capable of mutual recognition, love and lifelong commitment. But for this to happen we must be living according to the logic of God, in the certainty that he cannot mislead us, that he will not take advantage of our good will to send us off in some other direction.

In the meantime, all we have to do is continue faithful in our duty towards our neighbour, loving him or her with all our heart, with all our strength and with all our mind, trying not to look at every neighbour of the opposite sex as a possible soul-mate, but calmly awaiting that meeting which is bound to come. The evidence of my own eyes convinces me that for those who trust sincerely in the love of God, romance is not dead.

XVII
Risky Choices

M any couples begin married life thinking they know all there is to be known about each other and that everything has been sorted out between them, but how wrong they are! They have little idea of their own and each other's limitations, and as soon as these begin to make themselves felt, living together begins to seem impossible.

If only they had shown some common sense beforehand, and been willing to spend time getting to know each other properly, the dangers could have been foreseen. After weighing the risks carefully they would have said, 'This is going to be hard, but we think we're doing the right thing so we'll risk it. There are bound to be troubles, but if we stick together we'll succeed.' With such determination to overcome their difficulties, even serious ones, and being ready to admit their own limitations, they would have been assured of a happy and lasting marriage.

But if they insist on pretending that everything is just fine, and refuse to see each other as they really are, the end cannot be far off. When the honeymoon period is over they will awaken to the cruel truth, all the less bearable for having been denied so long. They will feel deceived and resentful, grievances will be multiplied, and their happy fantasy will lie in ruins.

Uncertainty is a fact of life and woe to those who refuse to accept it. Every commitment is accompanied by some risk, and a commitment to each other for life by two young people is very risky indeed. I wonder whether it is any less risky than the commitment to stay unmarried in order to follow Jesus.

The risks are not of course strictly comparable because they are not of the same kind. Following Jesus is dangerous because it entails in some sense going against the law of nature, the very law which was implanted in us by Jesus himself. He will ask us to give up those natural supports on which we depend for emotional and psychological security. Deep questions will remain to be sorted out, and they will present themselves to us later in all their sharpness. But let us not fool ourselves. Choosing is always difficult, and staying faithful to our choice, whatever it is, is always hard. Refusing to keep our eyes open can only make things worse.

XVIII
Being happy and making others happy

One useful test when we are trying to discover our vocation is to ask whether such and such a course will give us the best chance of being happy ourselves and making others happy. It is a simple idea, but we do not always remember it when we should, because the very idea of vocation is associated in our mind with thoughts of charitable work, striving after good, and various kinds of self-denial.

Of each new plan, ask the question: 'Is this the way that I shall be happy and make others happy?' If the answer is no, then either you have not found your vocation, or you have not yet fully understood what it entails, in which case this is not the right time to decide. Suppose you are in love with a girl and say to yourself, 'If I marry her, I am not sure of being happy myself or of making her happy.' Then you should wait a bit longer before deciding. Delay is advisable because the necessary foundation for a good marriage is lacking. In the same way, you do not apply to the seminary simply out of a desire to please your headmaster or parish priest. If you are not sure that you will be happy yourself and make others happy it is better to postpone the decision. This criterion is only common sense, but we often forget it.

XIX
Nothing is Lost

Jesus can call us into a state of life far removed from our original expectations, and in the course of getting there we may be required to sacrifice some of our gifts for the benefit of other people, whom we may not even have met. But it is striking to see how Jesus always respects our integrity as persons. Talents that have become secondary for us still have value for him, because they are part of our personality. What we have given up and forgotten is often returned much later with interest, if only for a short while.

This point is well illustrated by a passage in the gospel. The disciples, having long ago left their ordinary trade of fishing to become 'fishers of men', meet Jesus after he has risen from the dead, and once again, after all this time, he enables them to make a miraculous catch. It is in fact the sign by which they recognize him.

Those who have left all to follow Jesus and have come, through a long and faithful discipleship, to a state of life which they could never have foreseen when they were young, lose nothing of their true self. Their glorious exploits for the Church and the world spring from the whole personality, every talent being called by Jesus into his service, including even some which might once have seemed faults, but which now, healed by love, are revealed as also useful in building up the kingdom.

XX

You, follow me!

Towards the end of St John's Gospel Jesus asks Peter three times, 'Do you love me more than the others?' And three times he strengthens him in his vocation, which is to care for the Church. Then he prepares Peter for what will happen to him when he is old. 'When you were young you dressed yourself as you pleased and went wherever you wanted, but the day will come when others will fasten your belt and lead you where you do not wish to go.' And then John adds, 'Jesus said this to show Peter by what sort of death he would bear witness to God.'

Peter, on hearing these words, turns and particularly notices John. Having just been confirmed in his vocation as guide and supporter of his brothers, he has a certain responsibility for the other disciples, especially for John, the youngest. So he asks Jesus, 'What will become of John?' And Jesus replies tersely, 'What is that to you? If I want him to wait until I come again, that is no business of yours. You, follow me!'

It is true that our lives are bound up together, and that we can help one another to be faithful to our vocation, but it is even more true that we have a personal relationship with Christ and that he wants us to follow him without worrying too much about what our friends are doing. Jesus did not wait until all the twelve were ready so that he could call them all at the same time. Jesus says, 'Your choice, your decision, is no one's business but yours, and that person's choice is no one's business but his or hers. Don't wait for someone else to make up his mind before deciding yourself. You, follow me!'

What strikes us about the way Jesus called his disciples is that he did not call them in batches, but one by one, personally. He emphasizes the point when he says, almost callously, 'What business is it of yours? Do what you have to do, and leave the others alone.'

XXI
The Typical Disciple

There is no such thing as the typical disciple. If we thought there were a category of persons who were fit to follow Jesus, we might be tempted to exclude the rest by definition, but it is clear from the gospel that this would be quite wrong. If Jesus shows any preference at all, it is for those who assume that they are incapable or unworthy of following him, the poorest and least important people. Even so, when someone who is rich and powerful and profoundly spiritual asks Jesus how to be perfect, Jesus is deeply moved and loves that individual in a personal way. Jesus never puts people into categories. You do not need to be penniless, simple-minded or inadequate to follow Jesus. You are just as eligible if you are rich, intelligent and in perfect health.

XXII

Vocations and Vocations

God has both created us and arranged a final rendezvous for us, which is paradise, or eternal life. Although the destination is the same for all, the routes by which we get there are many and varied, because God has given us complete freedom. We can see two forces at work in our lives as they unfold, his call and our freedom, and these two are held in a mysterious balance by God's love.

Some vocations might be classified as earthly, because they are concerned with earthly means and needs, whilst others are more strictly related to eternal life. But as every believer knows, all vocations, earthly or otherwise, have a supernatural purpose. The vocations of a doctor or teacher are earthly, in the sense that they are a response to the needs of this world, but they ought to have a supernatural side as well, which is the desire to love God in one's neighbour.

On the other hand there are vocations to the religious life and the priesthood. A good deal has been said in recent years about the priestly vocation, and we can sum it up by saying that the priest is called mainly to communicate the grace of God through the sacraments, while the religious is called to leave everything and serve God alone, which includes God in the neighbour.

Every one of us has a vocation, a responsibility to use our physical, intellectual, psychological and other talents in the service of others as creatively as possible, but it is not always easy to know what this means in practice. Our vocation may demand great exertion, even danger, but we must use our talents faithfully, going to the limit of our ability in the service of others, not being content with small achievements which cost us little. Believers, it seems to me, have an advantage here, for when we undertake anything new or dangerous there are sources of spiritual strength which we can draw on when our progress is impeded by doubts or discouragement, or the misunderstanding of other people.

And here I should like to point out a trap into which believers can so easily fall when they are thinking about their future careers. They are tempted to opt instinctively for some kind of humanitarian work, whereas if they really considered the things they are good at they might go in for scientific research, business, music, the theatre, motor racing, politics, astronomy or physics, but as it is, all these fields end up abandoned to atheist ideologies or money-worship. Christianity meanwhile is regarded as an old-fashioned but respectable institution concerned only with charity and upholding moral values. We must claim our rightful share of all kinds of responsibilities in society, and refuse to be pigeon-holed in ways which do not fit our personality, much less the message of Christ.

So much for earthly vocations. But if God calls us explicitly to be occupied in the business of his kingdom he may well ask us to leave our work on one side, and to leave also the other responsibility we have as human beings, that of procreation. Then we enter the realm of the alternative logic, and the word 'vocation' acquires a more radical meaning. We shall be faced with choices which presuppose on our part a supernatural faith in God's love for us. The final rendezvous is in a sense brought nearer, for now we are planning our life with direct reference to eternal truths, believing more in the invisible things which we see with the eyes of faith than in those which we perceive with our senses.

We may think, and often, alas, with good reason, that following Jesus is like an ordinary profession. Instead of going in for medicine, say, we decide to be a priest, or to join a teaching or nursing order. The priesthood is considered more useful, essential even, and is open only to those who are called to it; and it happens that one of the conditions for being a priest (which incidentally applied until recently to air hostesses as well) is to be unmarried; but following Jesus, whilst being in some way more useful than other professions, on a higher level perhaps, is nevertheless not different in kind, but a sort of promotion. And this deplorable and persistent confusion misses the whole point. There are vocations and vocations. We can follow an earthly vocation as a doctor, a biochemist, a roadsweeper, or whatever it might be, in response to the call of Jesus, and live that vocation in such a way that it witnesses to the kingdom of heaven. If, on the other hand, we have been called to a ministry in the Church or to membership of a religious community, it is essential not to confuse the work we do with the vocation itself.

The important thing when we follow Jesus, is to follow him. Afterwards he may call us to perform some special service for his community of believers. It seems to me that one of the main reasons for the present desperate shortage of religious and priestly vocations is a crisis of identity: if you can serve the needs of children just as well by being a married teacher as by being a nun, why become a nun? But we are confusing the work the teacher does with the state of being a nun, and forgetting that the usefulness of the nun consists above all in being a nun, that is a woman consecrated to God.

The call to follow Jesus is a call to intimacy and trust, a call to share his responsibility for the kingdom of heaven, which is not of this world, but exists within it. We may find ourselves having both to follow our vocation to intimacy with Jesus, to share in his responsibility for the kingdom of heaven, and our human responsibility in society, to which equally we belong. In the case of a teaching nun, wanting to teach does not in itself create a vocation to be a religious, any more than the religious vocation automatically makes a good teacher. There are children whom, for various reasons, society has neglected to educate, whom no one will wish to teach except someone who is motivated by the pure love of God and neighbour. Jesus may lead such a person, who is on intimate terms with himself, to put his or her human talents (in this case teaching skills) at the service of these forgotten children. But we must distinguish clearly between the vocation to the religious life and the profession which he or she exercises.

The only way we shall solve the crisis in vocations is by tackling the real question head-on. Jesus can call absolutely anybody, and if he calls let us follow wherever he leads.

He will show some that the way for them to serve the kingdom of heaven is by staying in their own profession. He will need others to serve him in other countries, and others to serve him as priests. There are many rooms in his Father's house.

XXIII
The Parable of the Talents

What is the connection, if any, between earthly vocation and supernatural vocation? A well-known parable in the gospel tells us precisely. A rich man was due to set out for a far country to be made king. As he would be away a long time he called together various people whom he could trust to look after his financial affairs. Taking into account their different abilities he gave one servant five talents which was a large sum of money. To another less able he gave two, and to another only one.

After this he went off to receive his crown, and after a long absence he came back to reckon with his servants. The one who had received five talents said, 'You gave me five talents, and here are five more which I have earned for you.' In the same way the man who had received two talents gave him back four. But the man who had received only one talent said bitterly, 'You are hard in your dealings, you harvest where you have not sown, and I was afraid I should not be able to give back all that is yours. So I buried the talent you gave me in the ground. Here it is, count it. It's all there. We are quits.'

The newly enthroned king said to the man who had given

him back ten talents, 'You have been faithful in small things so I will trust you with great ones. Enter into the joy of your master.' Another version of the parable specifies that he made him governor of ten cities. The man who had given back four talents was made governor of four. But to the faint-heart he said sternly, 'I will condemn you out of your own mouth. You said I was a hard man, even a cheat. You knew what to expect. You could have put my money in the bank. It would have cost you nothing, you would have risked nothing, and you would not have needed to lift one finger on my account, but my money would have earned interest. You did not even do that, so much the worse for you!'

If I have understood correctly, the man whom the master had entrusted with five talents, and who, thanks to his industry, had gained five more, was allowed to keep the whole lot, together with the bonus of his colleague's one talent, and on top of that was given the governorship of ten cities. The servant who had made his two talents bear fruit also received an important charge. But the man who was lacking in character, who had no confidence in himself or in life, or in the talent that had been entrusted to him, failed to develop even that little bit of personality which he had.

This is the point of the parable as I see it. Everyone is endowed with ability. We have received a bundle of inherited capacities, which are supplemented by those we acquire from society, and these cards are dealt out quite differently according to continent, nation, society, sex, family, and even according to position within the family. What we are given at the start is not evenly shared out. God knows our varied capabilities and trusts us with different tasks, giving us one, two or five talents. In other words, if we want to understand what our role in society is to be, we must first examine the talents we have been given, see what our capabilities are.

Some people examine their responsibilities, take appropriate action, and devote their energy to their human vocation. Others, unnerved by the responsibility, give up and refuse to make their God-given talents bear fruit. They pretend to be busy with their own affairs, saying they won't be pushed about, but the truth is that they are afraid of failure. Discouraged before they even begin, they turn their backs on the struggle, saying no to life. Now each of us is truly necessary to others, we all matter to one another. Even though we may seem to have little to give, it is only we who can give it, and if we fail, others will be impoverished.

The problem is a real one. Children born into rich or powerful families are sometimes allowed, even if they are clever, to avoid responsibility and take life easy. We may be endowed with intelligence, strength or skill, but, through either laziness or false humility, we content ourselves with a mediocre life, taking no chances. But then God (or our conscience) seeks a reckoning. If we have been faithful, if we have made our talents bear fruit, God will say, 'You have been faithful in small things, I will entrust you with great things.'

This is where we find the supernatural vocation, the call to follow Jesus. If we have been faithful in our human life, if we have shown that we have matured, that we are capable of taking responsibility, that we have developed early in life all our potential abilities, that we have cultivated all the possibilities which we have discovered within ourselves, intellectual, physical, emotional, and spiritual (because that is also a dimension of human life) then Jesus will say, 'You have been faithful to yourself, you have become yourself, you are a balanced personality, but what you know about yourself at this moment is very little compared with what you mean to me. You have done all this for yourself, and you are proud of what you have achieved by your own efforts, your intelligence and your perseverance, for you have doubled your investment. I do not see you as merely a steward of my wealth. I see you as capable of governing a city.' And that is something entirely different. The king in the parable did not say, 'I am going to entrust you with ten thousand talents,' but, 'Since you have been faithful in looking after my wealth, in an ordinary private capacity, I believe you are ready to be launched into public life, to become a governor.'

The move from faithful steward to governor is not simply promotion; the kinds of responsibility are quite different. It is the same when Jesus tells Peter that he will no longer catch fish but people. There comes a time when an essential change takes place, and it is no longer a matter of developing our human talents. From now on Jesus, looking at us with love, sees us differently.

The man who left for a far country to be made a king already knew that when he returned he would have to choose governors for the cities of his new kingdom. On whom could he rely, if not those persons who, when they had complete control of his wealth, showed themselves to be honest and resourceful? So before he left, he conferred on his servants the greatest responsibilities of which they were capable, and when he returned he had the satisfaction of observing that two had done well. They had passed the test to which he had secretly subjected them.

Alas for the man who was afraid, for he also had been sounded out, and been judged capable of looking after one talent. If he had lived up to his responsibility the master had planned to make him governor of two cities. But he had not dared or tried to be fully himself, and he was left with nothing. He had not developed himself. No one would rely on him again, even in small things.

If we are to be able to ask God, 'Is there anything else you want us to do?' we must first prove that we are capable of carrying out the responsibility he has already given us, of fulfilling our human personality. Then God can say, 'Yes, I can see more in you. Now you may participate in the humanity of Jesus, who is fully human, but also God.' Jesus is now ready to share his divine life with us, and, by means of our complete dedication to him, we can communicate it to others. Having succeeded to his kingdom he will entrust us with a share of his responsibility, if, that is, we have been faithful in small things. Otherwise he will ask nothing more of us.

XXIV

Is Marriage a Vocation?

We have seen that there is no necessary contradiction between marriage and the call to enter the service of Jesus in the kingdom of heaven on earth. Jesus says that we must leave father, mother, brothers, sisters, wife (or husband, though Jesus himself called only men), lands, and our own life, and take up our cross and follow him. So if we are married we can follow Jesus, provided that our husband or wife takes second place to God. This leaves room for the possibility of a true vocation to marriage.

In one sense we are all called to be married, and no one can be called by Jesus to celibacy if he or she does not feel called to marriage first. Otherwise, by thwarting an essential human instinct, we shall have buried a talent, as if to say: 'I want to follow God, therefore I must not marry. Therefore I keep my eyes off the girls. I am pure.' But God will demand a reckoning: 'How is this? I gave you the capacity for loving. I gave you emotions and sexuality. What have you done with them?' Not only will our vocation to virginity not be a true one, but we shall lack the proper dispositions for marriage, because our human nature is undeveloped. And he will take back the talent which we have refused to use fruitfully.

We cannot be called to follow God in the consecrated state of virginity unless we have fully developed our capacity for marriage. Then the time will come when God will be able to say, 'I can see in you the possibility of living your human life in a mysterious way, which is virginity.' Virginity is to marriage what the cities were to the talents in the parable, that is to say, of a different kind. It is a different way of living human life.

Can people be called to marriage? We should mention straightaway that some people hear the call of God when they already are married. Since they are sacramentally joined together, it must follow that their vocation can be fulfilled within the limits set by their marriage. God is not calling them to be divorced! Long tradition has made it hard for us to think of this type of vocation as genuine, but now there are many spiritual movements in which such vocations are common, and we have been forced to look at them seriously, and with respect, lest we be found to be opposing God. When you see how these married people live who are called by God to give themselves completely to him, you realize that their marriage is different. While they are living a marriage that is humanly perfect (as much as it is possible to be) they become aware that each must put the other in second place, take up their cross and follow Jesus. Another dimension is introduced to the marriage. On to a fruitful human talent God grafts something else which has a certain resemblance to virginity, but is lived within marriage, and therefore takes account of the sexuality of the couple, their responsibility towards their children, etc. Having been faithful in their human marriage, which is a relatively small – because earthly – thing, they are entrusted with something greater, which already belongs to paradise, and to the kingdom of heaven on earth.

Some people are called not only by natural instinct but by God to be married, because it is as married people that he wishes to entrust them with heavenly things. People like this will, I believe, in their sincere desire to serve Jesus within marriage, find someone else with whom that sort of marriage will be possible. It would be out of the question, within marriage, for either partner to go it alone, since the acceptance of the vocation will necessarily change the life of both, and both must therefore be agreed about it. The great difficulty about following a vocation within marriage is that decisions are no longer taken alone, but together, so it is necessary to marry someone with whom we shall be able to agree together to put God in first place. The marriage has not only a human dimension, but a divine one, for which each partner shares the responsibility. Most of us are called to be married, so we are called to make a human success of it, but we ought also as married people to bear in mind that Jesus may wish to call us to something even better, to set us apart for the building up of the kingdom. St Paul's advice is plain: 'You can marry, and there is no reason not to, but you must remember that if you marry you will owe a duty to your spouse, so you will be divided between God and your spouse. I would rather you avoided that.'

I know married people who have succeeded in being wholly with God, and I believe that many ought to try to be like them. Since so many marry, let them do it in such a way that they can follow Jesus in the married state. But it is possible only when they live their married life to its full human extent and when the couple each agree to take second place to God; and this is hard, because jealousy is one of the most generously distributed faults of the human race. We never admit that we are jealous of God, but then, we are not thinking of God as being in first place. We realize we are in second place, and keep wondering who the person in first place is. It takes great trust and great love to accept that it is God and not some other person, or work, or self-interest that is in first place. Such a marriage, to be successful, must be contracted between two people called by God, whom God has loved as a couple, even before they knew each other.

So I am convinced that some men and women are made for each other, to be happy together. But this will come out only if each is trying to follow God, holding nothing back. If we are faithful to our whole selves, including the spiritual side of our personality, and if we are meant to marry, we shall meet someone with whom it will be possible to continue to live for God. I think there are enough examples to show that this can happen.

XXV
Sharing His Life

Let our ideal be to do everything together with Jesus, and to do nothing unfit for his eyes to see. To say to him, when we begin anything new, 'I am doing this for you.' We need not be afraid to let him come with us wherever we go, to share our whole life. He will not disturb us or distract us from what we are doing.

He will be our companion, the sharer of our troubles, our weariness, our hopes, our joys and our disappointments. If we introduce him into our daily life, he will actually take part in it. If we open our heart to him, he will share our feelings, our distress and our enthusiasms. If we open our mind to him, he will share our searchings, our thoughts, our discoveries, our doubts and our certainties. If we open our will to him, he will share our hesitations and our decisions. If we open our soul, he will share our trials, our temptations, our humiliations and our failures, our pride in recovery. He will join in our prayers to the Father and will himself pray for our intentions.

From his personal experience Jesus understands our life and all that we go through. Having been young himself, he knows what it feels like to grow up. He knows what it is like to be tempted, to have friends, to weep, to rejoice, and to work with one's hands. It was so hard for him to accept God's will that he wept in agony and sweated drops of blood. He took pleasure in food and drink and enjoyed festivals. He experienced setbacks and sadness, loneliness and discouragement. 'He, being in the form of God, did not count equality with God a thing to be grasped, but emptied himself, taking the form of a servant, being born in the likeness of men, and was found in human form.' And now, Jesus, having shared our life, wants us to share his. As he was ready to live our human life and to die a death like ours, so now he wishes to communicate his risen life to us. Having willingly shared all our joys and labours, without shrinking from the suffering involved, he wishes us to share his heavenly joy. Having of his own free will gazed with us on the horizons of this world, he wishes to unveil before our eyes the horizons of his kingdom. He who needed no persuasion to enjoy the simple pleasures of daily life, wishes us to taste the joys of heaven. He who was not ashamed of human feelings, wishes to reveal the feelings of the heart of God.

Jesus lives our life, why not live his? If he comes to live with us, why should we not go to live with him? It is enough to ask him, like John and Andrew, and he will simply reply as he did to them, 'Come!'

Since Jesus listens with pleasure – and patience – to all our chatter, why not ask him what he wants to say to us? That is what prayer is. Because he associates himself with our plans, and is one with us in everything, why not make ourselves one with him, and set ourselves to carry out his plans? Since it is no shame to him to go with us everywhere, why not accompany him where he goes, without fear of what others will say? Are we not able to watch one hour with him, to be at the foot of the Cross and in the upper room at Pentecost, like John, who was the first to follow him to his house and wanted to stay with him? Or shall we be like the rich young man, and go sorrowfully away because of our worldly attachments? Shall we, to avoid sharing our little wealth with Jesus in the person of the poor, deprive ourselves of the great wealth that Jesus has stored up for us? Let us live with Jesus, and we shall grow to be like him, or rather, we shall become him, for it is to his own life that he wishes us to be joined. To be a Christian is to be Jesus, and for that new birth in the Spirit, of which Jesus spoke to Nicodemus, we have a mother, Mary. Let us ask her to bring us to birth in the life of Jesus.

XXVI
The Greatest Vocation

Which is the greatest vocation? 'Mine!' answers the Benedictine, quite truthfully. And the Carmelite, the Jesuit, the Little Brother of Jesus, Mother Teresa's Missionary of Charity all say the same. (And, speaking as a Focolarino, let me also say that my vocation is the greatest!) All of us are right. If we did not think our vocation was the greatest, how could it be a proof of God's personal love for us? But we must remember that all other vocations are just as excellent for those who are called to them. It would be worrying if anyone thought his or her vocation was greater than anybody else's. Each person's vocation is the greatest, not by comparison with others, but absolutely.

So all vocations are equally greater than one another, and all on the same level. If we can be convinced of the truth of this paradox we shall experience a new freedom in finding our own vocation. Rather than looking for the one that seems the noblest, and forcing ourselves to conform to it, we shall simply try to understand what God in his love has planned for us, convinced that, because it will be our vocation, it will be the best. In the meantime we can serenely admire the others without any feeling of jealousy, or disappointment because we do not feel cut out for a particular sort of dedication in our life.

Many people have a curious mental picture of vocations arranged in a sort of hierarchy, with certain forms of the contemplative life at the top, and the active life right at the bottom. Such a conception has the beauty of a flow chart, but is entirely misleading, and an insult to God's love for his chosen. Human nature loves comparisons, but Jesus rendered that sort of discussion pointless when, hearing his disciples wrangling about who was the greatest among them, he made them ashamed of such vanity and spoke to them of the only kind of primacy worth desiring, that of service. And lest this should tempt us to set up a new hierarchy, arranging the different types of service in order of merit, we must remember that the greatest and most heroic acts, if performed without love, are as nothing in God's eyes. Accordingly the traditional distinction between the state of perfection and ordinary life now seems somewhat quaint. What distinguishes saints is not the state of perfection they are in, but their perfect manner of life in that state to which they are called.

XVII
Too Much Choice

When we have become aware that Jesus is calling us to follow him by completely devoting our life to his service, we are often like Buridan's ass who was so hungry and thirsty that, although there was a pail of fresh water and a bag of oats within his reach, he died of hunger and thirst because he could not decide whether to eat or drink. With such a variety of attractive courses to follow, it is hard to choose any, since whichever prize we choose, we must give up another. But we have to remember that life consists of a series of choices, every one of which entails some sacrifice, which is sometimes painful and always necessary, because we cannot be everything at once.

As we have said before, to be a person at all means accepting our limitations, our particular circumstances. It means cutting through a mass of still muddled possibilities, and choosing something real, tangible and plain. Our personality develops as we increasingly emphasize the things that make us different, which are also limitations, and progressively rule out other developments that were originally possible. The further we advance through life, the more we commit ourselves in certain directions to the exclusion of others.

The discovery that we are finite is an extremely distressing experience, almost unbearable, because humankind feels a deep and irresistible longing for the infinite and the absolute. This is perhaps the human experience *par excellence*: to come to terms with the knowledge that we are creatures who are limited, and ever more limited, whilst at the same time to feel a growing awareness of the infinite and the absolute. As our physical and intellectual strength diminishes moment by moment through our adult life, we can feel some inner part of us growing, which we must encourage to develop fully, because that is all that will be left of us when earthly life is extinguished.

So as we go along, let us choose whatever best corresponds to our word of life, our inner self, that part of us which continues to grow as the rest declines.

We must choose between good and evil, certainly, and when we know that those are the alternatives the choice is relatively easy, because we shall always prefer the good. Even if the evil holds a fascination for us, the good will attract us more. It is true that we are influenced by original sin, as our faith calls it, but we must believe that if Christ was present in creation at the beginning, then grace, and not sin, is original.

However, we usually have to choose between one good and another, and we must remember that the good which God does not wish is an evil. We must therefore learn to recognize what is good for us, and give up those choices that are good for another person but evil for us, or at least less good, or relatively evil.

XXVIII
Different Roads

In the course of the Church's history the desire to answer the call to follow Jesus and live after the pattern of the gospel has led men and women along a great variety of roads. Each one is an intelligent and practical search for the way of perfection, and the person who perseveres in following it is led through all the stages of Christian life to the goal, which is common to all, of conformity to Christ.

These roads are not only different but mutually contradictory. A hermit has nothing in common with a monk, nor a monk with someone living a consecrated life while remaining in the world, nor a contemplative with an active religious. But the differences are more apparent than real, for we are all called to live according to the same gospel, and in the end the whole gospel, even if the ways into the gospel are so varied.

The great distinction we make between active and contemplative makes good sense when we consider the types of communities that came into being in answer to these two sorts of vocation. Strictly enclosed monasteries with austere rules on one hand, and on the other hand communities dedicated to the practical service of children, the sick, and the old.

Nothing could be more dissimilar. However, the enclosed monks are quite right to devote themselves to the one thing necessary, and since they have chosen the better part, it will not be taken away from them. By contrast, those men and women who have taken to heart the final judgement, which will be concerned, as we know, with practical charity, have understood that for Jesus nothing is small if it is done out of love. Their vocation too is very attractive.

By tradition the names of the two sisters of Lazarus, Jesus' friend, have been attached to these vocations, to remind us that completely different though they are, they can co-exist in the Church. Mary, who sat at Jesus' feet to listen to him, stands for contemplation. Martha, who busied herself with household tasks, and with welcoming and preparing a meal for Jesus and his disciples (who were not after all pure spirits) stands for activity.

Martha and Mary had different priorities, which corresponded with their temperaments, but living with Christ seems to have had a balancing effect on their personalities. When Lazarus is dead and Jesus visits the sisters at Bethany, it is Martha who comes to meet the master while Mary is busy with the funeral meal, so Martha resembles Mary. Her preoccupation with human needs has taught her that human beings do not live by bread alone, but by every word that proceeds from the mouth of God. And Mary also comes to resemble Martha, for she now realizes that though she might know the language of angels, if she did not have charity, it would profit her nothing.

In the same way it is remarkable that the woman who perhaps best symbolizes the contemplative vocation, Teresa of Avila, should have spent the last years of her life on the road founding reformed Carmels, and that another Teresa, of Calcutta, whose life is an outstanding example of practical charity, says that she has a vocation to the contemplative life because she sees Jesus in the dying and the sick whom she serves.

Similarly I believe that the difference between hermits and those who lead a consecrated life whilst staying in the world is more apparent than real. The strong argument of the hermits is that here we have no abiding city, that each successive day brings us nearer to our end, that our true life is the other one, where God will be all in all. So they conclude that the wisest course is to let go of the world straightaway, and retire to a desert place to begin here below that life which they will continue in the hereafter. They retreat from the world in order to attain to union with God, arguing that since the world is opposed to God, we should take God's side. Their way of perfection is a life of solitude ever more fully given to penitence and prayer.

There are others, however, who have felt the call to remain in the world, because they see that, by leaving the world, they would be leaving their fellow human beings, and that the way to God is by way of the love of their brothers and sisters. 'If anyone says that he loves God, whom he has not seen, and does not love his brother or sister whom he has seen, he is a liar.'

Jesus used to retire to the hills to pray, but he enjoyed the company of other people, and let them come to him. When a hermit has attained his goal and is living the life of paradise on earth, he will not be left alone for long, because others will be attracted to him by his peace and goodness. On the other hand, those whose vocation is to remain in the world will find that, by loving their neighbour and living in the world but not of it, they are not being separated from God by the world. On the contrary, the trials and persecutions which the world inflicts will enable them to progress rapidly on their way of perfection.

There are some vocations which offer a subtle combination of these contradictory elements. That at least is how I see my own vocation as a Focolarino, which consists in maintaining the presence of Jesus in the midst of the focolare[1] (contemplation) by means of mutual love which brings us into unity (action) in complete consecration to Jesus forsaken[2] (action and contemplation).

Contemplation and action, flight from the world or involvement in the world, two very different ways. We must choose. Each one is beautiful, and when we choose one we exclude the other. But if we choose well, and if we are faithful to our choice, we shall all arrive at the end of the road, at that rendezvous to which all roads lead, eternal life.

[1] A small community at the heart of the wider community of the Focolare Movement. (Ed.)
[2] Jesus who, dying on the Cross, cried out: 'My God, my God, why have you forsaken me?' (Ed.)

XXIX
Virginity

I have read that St Ambrose spoke so eloquently and persuasively about virginity, that the Milanese tied up their daughters to prevent them from listening to the saint and being 'made' virgins. The expression is a curious one, for virginity is commonly thought of as something that can be lost or kept, surely not acquired or made, but on reflection I find it particularly appropriate. We need to get away from the common attitude and try to understand what virginity means in the context of our consecration to God. It is certainly not a matter of preserving something earthly of extraordinary value, for there is no earthly reason for remaining a virgin. In the realm of earthly life virginity is inferior to motherhood or fatherhood. Being called to celibacy is not the same as being a permanent child. This somewhat mocking term clearly cannot refer to virgins who are consecrated to that state. No, virgins are not trying to preserve something. They are not people who refuse to emerge completely from adolescence, and keep themselves in a state of immaturity. Virginity is not an incapacity for marriage and sexuality, or a rejection of them. The motive for virginity can be found only in heaven. And what does

Jesus tell us about heaven? That in heaven, although we shall live in our bodies, there will be no marrying or giving in marriage, and we shall be like the angels. In heaven we shall be complete, no longer beings who lack something essential, needing the other sex in order to be whole. We shall still be men and women, because our earthly life has been lived in a body whose every cell bears the imprint of sex, but we shall be like Jesus and Mary, with nothing lacking in our human nature.

Jesus is undoubtedly a man and Mary is undoubtedly a woman, and we can see from their personalities that they lack nothing which the other sex finds beautiful. Jesus, however, whose manliness is undeniable, and perhaps precisely because of that, declares without shame that he is meek and lowly of heart. He weeps publicly for his friend Lazarus and over Jerusalem, which he has so ardently desired to gather as a hen gathers her chicks under her wings. When he wants to describe the fatherhood of God he uses the illustration of the prodigal son's father, and attributes to him the heart of a mother. These examples of Jesus' femininity, if the word can be used without misleading, could be multiplied.

Mary for her part is the essential woman, with whom all feminine vocations can easily identify, sometimes showing strength, independence and other characteristics we might consider manly. And yet it is these qualities we want to magnify in her when we speak of her as the Virgin. We see the woman, strong, standing at the foot of the cross, and again holding her dead son in her arms, the woman without a man, not so much because she is a widow and her son is dead, but because from the very beginning she has belonged only to God and has known only God.

When the angel invites her to become the mother of the Messiah, she is astonished because she does not yet know a man, but she accepts this miraculous motherhood all by herself, without telling even Joseph, who would also have to learn to depend on God alone.

So we can see that the vocation to virginity is a profound mystery, belonging to the heavenly realm, nothing less than a gift of God. In Christian marriage humanity reaches the closest resemblance to the creator of which it is capable – St Paul dares to claim that the love of husband and wife is the image of that of Christ for his Church – but the vocation of virginity is the life of heaven already lived on earth. We say that it has a prophetic or eschatological character, meaning that those who are called to it are bearing witness by their life to the transitoriness of earthly life.

Our sexuality is the mark upon us of belonging to time and space, while virginity is the pledge here and now that we belong to the future, eternal world. Marriage reminds us that the love of God is lived in all the most provisional circumstances of human life. Virginity by simply existing points to another dimension, telling us again and again that this world with all its beauty will pass away. In our life which is dying, virginity is the seed of the life which will never die, and is experienced as the result of taking the word of Christ literally, 'Whoever saves his life shall lose it, and whoever loses his life for my sake (for the sake of the kingdom of heaven) shall find it.'

The gospel prefers the state of virginity because it is an experience that prefigures the state of life of the blessed, although the two states are entirely different. In our earthly life here and now virginity is experienced in a person's inner sexual life, but in the future life, everything will be totally renewed by the resurrection. In the gospel, virginity is seen as a form of apostolic service: the virgin is more available for the Church's work. Virginity is not an end in itself, but is a means to service and witness, and since it is a means and not an end, the Church officially recognizes the commitment. However, virginity is valued by the Church not primarily because it makes people more available to do the Church's work, but because it witnesses to the power of God. Virginity is a living message for all Christians, because we can see the virgin's faith in the power of God who is at work in the personality. By this faith the virgin can live in the poverty of him who gave up everything, and in his weakness, his solitude, and his renunciation of earthly success and of having descendants. The virgin knows that God will save his or her life, and waits for him to raise it up, living in intimacy with him, who is the sole support and husband of the soul, as the mystics say.

So virginity is not simply a decision to stay unmarried in order to be more available for apostolic labour. It is a gift of God, a charism, that is a gift not restricted to the person who receives it, but destined, through him or her, to be communicated to the whole Church. It is a gift which God bestows with sovereign freedom. If we have not received the gift ourselves, it is pointless to worry; we are simply being told that we shall show God's love to the world by our fulfilment in human love. But if we have received this gift, if we feel we can take Christ's words literally and leave everything, even husband or wife, even ourselves, to follow Jesus, let us be clear in our minds that we are under no compulsion to do it, but that our response must be fundamentally free. And let us remember that the gift is not for our benefit but that of the Church, which will receive it only if we exercise our freedom to accept the call.

XXX
The Virgin Family

It is not good for man to be alone, and God calls us all to some kind of family life, either natural, as in most cases, or supernatural, as in the case of those called to virginity. And this is in keeping with the nature of God, who is himself a family, and whose incarnate Son was brought up in a family, commonly known as the Holy Family. As it consisted of virgins it was a very special family, but one which seemed ordinary enough to everybody round about, so that when Jesus began to preach and work his first miracles, his fellow-citizens could not believe their eyes and said to one another, 'We know him, he is the son of Joseph, the carpenter.' The life of the family must have appeared quite normal, otherwise these good folk would have said, 'I'm not surprised. I always thought there was something odd about their goings-on. And don't you remember the rumours that went round when Jesus was born?'

But there was nothing of the sort. The special vocation of the three members of the family passed completely unnoticed. No one suspected anything. There was nothing in their way of life to attract attention. They were not ostentatious in their piety. Morally they were neither puritanical nor loose-living. They were neither on the fringe of their society nor were they leaders of it. Jesus had not been forbidden by his parents to mix with the other children and young people of Nazareth. Their family was not well off, but neither did they live in abject poverty: besides, Joseph, although not occupying a position of privilege, was well established as a skilled worker in his own right, and of course taught his trade to his son. All the members of the family were content to follow the traditional customs. They needed no persuading to take part in the village festivals, at which we can imagine Jesus displaying a talent for singing and dancing, taking after his distant ancestor David.

So Jesus belonged to a proper family, one with a father – otherwise Freud would never have allowed us to forget the fact. A family to all appearances so normal that the vocation of each member could develop unobtrusively under the eye of God. A supernatural family with all its members dedicated to God and involved in a very special way in the working out of God's plan for the human race. Each one was a virgin, i.e., entirely free and responsible, able to hear the word of God and to act upon it. Each in turn, as occasion required, would be the one to whom God spoke, according to the particular task to be performed. Mary all by herself had taken on the miraculous conception of Jesus, leaving Joseph to sort out the matter with God and to play his own allotted part. When the threat of massacre hung over the child, it was Joseph, the official head of the family, who was warned in a dream, and in the middle of the night took the decision to set out and seek refuge in a foreign land. Incidentally, there is a point here of psychological interest: whilst Mary, the woman and therefore usually more passive, was visited by the angel in broad daylight, Joseph, who as a man would tend to be more active, was visited by the angel in his sleep. This testifies to the completeness of human nature in each of them, and also indirectly to their virginity. As for Jesus, as we have seen, he clearly demonstrated his independence and his close rapport with the Father at the age of twelve.

If this was the sort of family God chose for his Son, it is safe to predict that he intends something like it for his adopted children, those who renounce the formation of a natural family in order to follow Jesus. In fact, the group that formed round Jesus was of this kind. It was uphill work to make this assortment of rough and ready men into the new family of Nazareth, but that was his essential purpose: to make them brothers. And when he opened his heart to them during their last meal together, he gave them only one commandment, that of loving one another just as he had loved them. And a little later, when he addressed his last solemn prayer to the Father, he asked that his disciples might be one, in the very likeness of God; in other words, that they should be one supernatural family, 'so that their joy may be perfect.'

For all who are called to follow him in the state of virginity, Jesus has prepared a family in the likeness of his own, whose members are all virgins. It is precisely because they are virgins, wishing to know only God and able to do without the support of natural family life, that they are capable of living with others called to the same state. Their own family life, simple and open, joyful and uncomplicated, is actually a safeguard of their virginity, but does not seem restrictive or inhuman to other people living around, because it is so happy. It is easy to forget that they are not exactly like other people, because happiness is what we are all looking for, and when we come across it we are inclined simply to be glad, without probing beneath the surface.

These virgin families are known by various names: monasteries, convents, communities, brotherhoods, focolares. Their customs and rules are sometimes difficult for outsiders to understand, and someone who does not share the same vocation is bound to get an outsider's view, but there is no denying the fascination they hold for people. Some communities of women have undertaken such tough assignments as might have been thought by some to be beyond their powers, whilst there are communities of men who look after children or old people with a tenderness that is truly maternal. In the state of virginity love takes on subtleties of expression which in another setting would seem incongruous.

Pure disinterested love seeks nothing in return but God alone. It concentrates on loving the other as he or she needs to be loved, loving in the way which is right for that individual at this particular moment. The love of husband and wife may be excluded, but to make up for it, all the other kinds of love are experienced in turn: that of son or daughter, father, mother, brother or sister; so the promise is fulfilled, that those who have left everything to follow Jesus receive back a hundredfold, even in this life. And this supernatural family – fathers, mothers, brothers, sisters and children – is a foretaste of the eternal life that awaits them.

XXXI
Finding our Family

W hen we are sure that God has called us to virginity, we must then find the family he means us to live in. Some people would put it the opposite way and say that finding the spiritual family often comes first, before any vocation is felt, especially a vocation to virginity; and then through this meeting with the spiritual family, Jesus converts us, encourages us to follow him, and finally shows us exactly where our vocation is leading. So in what order does it really happen? It is the age-old puzzle of the chicken and the egg. The chicken comes out of the egg, and the egg comes from the chicken. By spiritual family I mean here a community that someone joins for life. The right one ought not to be too hard to find, because there must be some signs to show whether we are on the right track. Members of a natural family are characterized by ties of blood, resemblances in appearance and behaviour, shared tastes, habits, tricks of speech, a whole inheritance in common, and it is much the same with a supernatural family.

It always comes as a surprise to me to hear that the search for a spiritual family has been long drawn out. I wonder whether people who have to search for so long might not have taken a wrong turning and be looking far afield for something which is all the time close at hand. Or perhaps they have cut too many corners; before looking for the spiritual family they perhaps ought to have made sure that they really have chosen God, and that God is calling them to virginity; because otherwise the search is doomed to failure.

Everything hinges on following Jesus and understanding where he is leading us. Where, for our purposes, is Jesus' house? Come and see! Which spiritual family is right for us? Where do we feel happiest and most at home? Can we picture ourselves there seeking advice, correction or encouragement, and sharing the joys or troubles that are too great for us to bear alone? Where, in short, can we find Jesus? – because *there* will be our spiritual family. We shall not need to look elsewhere. But before we do anything else we must make sure that we really are members of that family, and for this three simple tests are enough. First, that we have the desire; secondly, that we are capable of living like that; and thirdly, that the members of that family accept us as belonging to them.

Desire, yes of course, because a vocation is not an act of pure generosity, a blind renunciation, a sort of spiritual kamikaze. There must be a positive desire to join that family, a profound sense that we are destined to find true happiness there. We must be convinced that this spiritual family offers the possibility of complete self-fulfilment along with the best opportunity of living our word of life. We must find the members of the community likeable, and even their faults not unattractive. We are, after all, talking about a commitment for life, and that is a long time. There will be times of testing, temptation and discouragement, but at the moment of deciding to join a spiritual family for life, the feeling of joy ought to be paramount. The life to which we are called will be sometimes demanding and harsh, and will entail sacrifices of various kinds, including a break with our natural family, but following Jesus and finding our spiritual family must always be essentially joyful.

Joining a spiritual family is not a marriage of convenience but a love match, when the two lovers are protected from the knowledge of their future troubles by their joy in the present. There will be time enough after the honeymoon to take stock of the less congenial aspects of their life together. Then they will remember that the call to virginity is at heart a call to solitude, and strengthened by this thought they will be enabled to make a contribution to the family in a way that accords with its special spiritual character, but in all its freshness, as in the glimpse they had when God originally called them there.

And we ought to be capable of the life. We may be fascinated by the prospect of living under vows, but if after serious self-examination, casting aside any preconceived ideas, we conclude that we are incapable of living like this, then the answer is simple: the life is not for us. There is no need for anxiety or self-interrogation or self-reproach; if we are called to a spiritual family, it must by definition match our capacities. It is supposed to help us in following Jesus, not hinder us. Perhaps we have been carried away by romantic feeling, or by the search for what we imagine to be a superior way of offering ourselves. Then, if we are frank, we shall realize that it is something within ourselves, and not Jesus, which has drawn us to this form of life. If we follow Jesus, and only him, he will lead us where he wishes, and we shall lose nothing, of that we may be sure.

Finally, we must be accepted by the members of the family. That goes without saying. Entry into a religious community requires, no less than marriage, the partner's consent. When two people marry it is enough for them to be in agreement, then they will form a new family. But in the case of the spiritual family, the new member must provide some evidence that he or she is called to it, because the family already exists. The existing members will need to recognize in the candidate the signs of their family, which has inherited a special character, the charism, or spiritual gift, proper to its founder, and which possesses its own tradition, which may go back for centuries. New members must prove that they have within them the seeds of the same charism, and be recognized by their future brothers or sisters as one of them, having the same spiritual blood flowing in their veins. Otherwise they will be foreign bodies and the graft will not take; and meanwhile, until rejection occurs, they will be a potential danger to the community that has rashly accepted them.

XXXII

The Vocation of Parents

Parents of a young person seeking to know his or her own vocation are often faced with a great deal of perplexity and unease. All their patience and common sense will be needed to help their child through this period, when silence and unobtrusiveness are likely to carry more influence than advice or reproaches. It seems to me that the biggest problem is that while the young person is not yet fully mature, going through all the difficulties of adolescence – questionings, doubts, enthusiasms and changes of mood – he or she runs the risk of taking a wrong turning that will only lead to unhappiness, and this naturally makes parents anxious. Their chief concern is to ensure that their child will be happy, and if they cannot imagine a particular course making for happiness they will put a spoke in the wheel. But when they are satisfied that their child has sufficiently matured and no undue pressure is being brought to bear – if, in a word, their child is happy – all objections will melt away and they will be proud of whatever way of life is chosen.

But if I may give a word of advice to young people about how to deal with their parents it would be to say: remember it is your future that must be settled, not that of your parents, so the problem is ultimately yours to solve. If, when you speak to your parents about it, you sound like a wayward child, rather than a reasonable adult, don't be surprised if they try to dissuade you. It would be better to put off talking to them until you have sorted out your difficulties and can convey to them the light and joy of following Jesus, rather than your doubts and the wrench of the sacrifices you must make.

Ideally parents ought not to suffer because of their child's vocation, but should feel only joy at seeing him or her happy and fulfilled. We know only too well that the final separation from a grown up child is nearly always painful and difficult, *a fortiori* if the vocation overturns long cherished plans, which may have cost a lot of money or demanded great sacrifices. But the parents of a young person whom Jesus calls have a vocation too. Think of Joseph, who certainly had no idea where his wife's vocation would lead, but proved he was able to help her. His vocation was to shape his life according to the requirements of her vocation. When Jesus calls a young person to leave his or her parents there is a corresponding implicit call to the parents to let their child go. The call is imposed on them by their child, and they may not be ready for it, but experience teaches us that Jesus' promise comes true, that those who leave anything for him will receive a hundredfold reward. From among the members of their child's new spiritual family parents will find many new children whom they can love and cherish in the same way as they loved the child who left them to follow Jesus.

Parents are rightly proud when they have allowed their child to become an adult, then an equal, a sort of brother or sister. They are, or they ought to be, overjoyed if their child is called to virginity, for then they have a child who is really independent, truly adult, and able to love them in such a way that they feel more like children of their child, and so truly equal.

It is now that the first prayer taught by parents to their children takes on its full significance, which they repeated without always realizing the depth of the mystery which these words contain: 'Our Father, who art in heaven . . . ' It is the announcement of what lies in the distant future but must inevitably come about, that parents and children together will be children of the same Father, and brothers and sisters one of another.

XXXIII
Under Sentence of Death

After reading the two large volumes of *The Gulag Archipelago* a few years ago, all I remember of Solzhenitsyn's work is one short paragraph, but for me it sums up the experience of the labour camps. I believe it is also the message of his masterpiece, *One Day in the Life of Ivan Denisovich*. If ever there was a message of hope, this is it. Solzhenitsyn explains that, in order to survive systematic persecution in a totalitarian state, it is necessary, from the moment of arrest, to think of yourself as dead, without family, friends, interests, attachments, or anything at all which might give others any hold over you. Any concern you may have for parents, brothers, sisters, spouse, children, friends, ideals, career, reputation, above all for self-preservation, will be manipulated by the authorities to wear down your resistance and get what they want out of you. The price of survival is to live like an orphan or like one without hope, indeed like one already dead; because the authorities are powerless in the face of someone who has nothing, not even life, to lose. They are disarmed, because their weapons are useless against you.

And this is the paradox: the powers that be are powerless

to harm the prisoner, and the prisoner is essentially free. The more the prisoner succeeds in being detached from everything and from self, the more free the prisoner is. Because of having decided beforehand to lose the battle, the prisoner is more certain of winning it. Solzhenitsyn learned this lesson from his own experience in the Soviet labour camps, but it applies equally in every struggle against totalitarianism. Your tormentors have power over you only if there is something still attaching you to life, someone they can make you weep for, some last treasure for which you can be lured into a compromise.

I was struck by the resemblance to the passage in the gospel where Jesus lays down the conditions for following him, 'If anyone would come after me, let him deny himself and take up his cross daily and follow me. For whoever would save his life will lose it; and whoever loses his life for my sake, he will save it.' And again, 'If anyone comes to me and does not hate his father and mother and wife and children and brothers and sisters, and even his own life, he cannot be my disciple.' We tend to find these conditions extreme, not to say excessive. But in the light of Solzhenitsyn's experience, we can see that they are not conditions laid down by Jesus himself, but a statement of plain sense, or as we might say, the advice of a friend. Moreover, Jesus goes on to say, if, despite all this, we set out to follow him without taking these essential precautions, we shall be objects of ridicule, like the king going unprepared into battle, or the man bankrupting himself building a tower.

Jesus does not present us with gratuitous or cruel tests in order to follow him. On the contrary, he advises us to assess the situation realistically, and not to commit ourselves under a romantic impulse to an undertaking that can end only in confusion and humiliation. Following Jesus means turning our back on the world. We must choose one or the other, for we cannot serve two masters. The world is incompatible with Jesus, and therefore with his disciples also. It will exert every possible compulsion to prevent us from being faithful to our choice of Jesus. It will behave like the totalitarian regime it is, asserting the right to control every aspect of human life. If we are to have any chance of resisting all its pressures, of which the deadliest are not the most brutal, Jesus gives us the same advice as Solzhenitsyn: deny yourself, consider yourself already dead, without spouse or children or any other attachment. Jesus is not jealous of our other attachments, but these are inevitably the means by which the world will bring pressure to bear, and at last wear down our resistance.

Jesus also says the disciple must, 'Take up his cross daily'. For Christians today the cross is nothing like the powerful symbol that it was for the hearers of Jesus; it was the instrument of capital punishment. To bring home the full force of Jesus's words we need to translate them into something like this: 'Every morning wake up your firing squad, and spend the day with them, waiting for your execution.' That is the state of mind which Jesus recommends to any one who wishes to follow him. We might regard this attitude as morbid, but another great Russian novelist, who had lived through just such an experience, explains that it is quite the opposite. Dostoevsky had been condemned to death and had seen his sentence commuted only at the last moment, when he was already on the scaffold, and he describes what he had been thinking at the time: 'If only I did not have to die! If only my life were to be given back to me! What an eternity would open before me! I would transform every minute into a century of life. I would not lose a single one, but would eke them out, not wasting any.' To know that we are condemned to death does not make us morbid, but on the contrary makes us value the moments of life that remain, so that we live them more intensely. That is what Jesus means: live as if condemned to die, in other words, not aimlessly, killing time, but as intensely as possible.

I remember a scene from the John Ford film *The Grapes of Wrath*. Henry Fonda, a young trade union leader, is meeting his mother for the last time. He is on the run after murdering a policeman, and he knows that if he is captured he will be killed. He is an outlaw, and as good as dead, and he will never see his mother again. But the fact of living under a suspended death sentence gives him complete freedom to devote the days or years that remain to the struggle for the rights of the oppressed. So where the fight for justice is, there he will be found, until the unknown but inevitable day when he will be taken and executed. Here we have an excellent picture of the follower of Jesus; as St Paul says, 'For him the world is like one condemned to death, and for the world he is like one condemned to death.' So having nothing to lose, he is completely free to be occupied with his Father's business.

XXXIV
Women Priests?

Is the priesthood a privilege confined to men? Or as most people might put it, have men a monopoly of power in the Church? Under pressure from the feminist movement the question is increasingly being asked, and invariably the traditional answer is yes, which is guaranteed to set many teeth gnashing. It is safe to predict that as long as the priesthood is seen as powerful (and the idea is unlikely to die out, since some power is legitimately attached to the priesthood) those men, and even more those women, who are not admitted to it will feel excluded, and will demand equal rights.

Of course I have no answer to the question whether one day women will be called to be priests, but what I can say is that vocation is a divine matter; it depends entirely on God; and God is supremely free. He can in this, as in so many other matters, make innovations as he pleases, so that what seems impossible today may by tomorrow have become quite normal. The same rule can be applied in every case: vocation is not just a personal feeling of being called, but something that requires confirmation by the Church. And this applies particularly to a vocation to the priesthood, where the final word lies, not with the individual who feels called, but with the whole Church.

The fact that women are claiming the right to become priests ought to make us think about an area of doctrine which has been little explored until now. The campaign itself may be a sign that God wants to prepare us for a change in the matter, and if that is so I believe we have to trust him. At the right moment, when the Church is ready for such a novelty, and when there has been a growth in understanding about the nature of the priesthood, she will call women in such a way that they will be able to convince the Church that their vocation is genuine. It is impossible to separate the Holy Spirit who calls, from the Holy Spirit who guides the Church and enables her to recognize a new vocation. If we do not believe this we shall fall into subjectivity, and so far from following Jesus, we shall be following our own inclinations. Going back to our question, 'Is the priesthood a privilege confined to men?' there is no denying that it is so at present, and always has been until now, and, to judge by the way things are going, will remain so for a long time yet. But is it really a privilege? We have to confess that the accusation is not without foundation. Clericalism is not, alas, a pure invention, as the priests themselves will all testify.

What ought to be the relationship between the priest and the Church? The answer in a word is, service, although I realize that this is often a convenient code word for 'power'. Before he instituted the priesthood, in order that his disciples should clearly understand what kind of authority he was about to give them, Jesus washed their feet. Although, the same evening, he confirmed Peter in his primacy, he had no illusions about Peter's reliability or about the worth of his protestations.

We shall understand the relationship between the Church and the priest a little better if we study the situation of Mary and John after the death of Jesus. The gospel tells us that Jesus whilst on the cross entrusted Mary and John to each other's care, and that John took Mary to his house. We notice particularly that Jesus not only entrusted his mother to John, saying, 'Behold your mother', but he also entrusted John to Mary, saying, 'Behold your son.' Mary, like all Christians, is entrusted to a priest, John, who is in a sense the head of Mary's spiritual family, and he takes her home as he is commanded. But in view of the youth of John and the sanctity of Jesus' mother, it would be more true to say that it was Mary who had taken him home with her. Very likely this is how it appeared to John himself. Through Mary he was begotten again to the life of Christ. That is why, when we read the gospel and letters of John we cannot help reading between the lines the gospel according to Mary, the gospel of love and light.

Whilst meditating on this mystery I painted a picture showing John giving Holy Communion to Mary. John appears overwhelmed by a mystery which completely passes his understanding, while Mary seems to be seeing far beyond the consecrated bread which she is taking from John's hands. Although he is giving it to her, it appears to belong more to her than to him. And that is how I imagine the relationship of the priest to the Church: the priest gives the Church nourishment for her Christian life, but the Church is the mother of the Christian life of the priest. And who exercises this spiritual motherhood in the Church? It is particularly women called to virginity, who for all sorts of reasons you could say are devoted to God in a more radical way than men. Isn't spiritual motherhood among women what the priesthood is among men? They are two equal vocations, two distinct kinds of privilege, as in the case of Mary and John, truly equal because they are two kinds of superiority, each respecting and reverencing the other.

XXXV
Maturity

In an ideal world we should not have to take any decisions which would affect our adult life until we were mature enough to gauge the consequences, and to know our own capacity for being faithful to our commitments; until, that is, we were capable of discernment. The trouble is that we are not like fruit that falls from the tree at a given moment when it is ripe. Our maturing is a lifelong and continuous process, so that there never will be a moment when we can say we are completely mature; there will always be something more to achieve if we want to measure up to the perfectly mature figure of humanity, 'the stature of the fullness of Christ', as St Paul says. However, common sense tells us that a certain degree of maturity is both necessary and possible for a young person on the threshold of adulthood. This maturity cannot altogether be defined, since it is more of a general condition, or style of life, but we need not therefore give up the attempt to describe it. We can say that in the maturing process there are certain stages at which we are able to exercise free and responsible choice, and there are certain criteria that allow us to judge fairly accurately how mature a person is.

One aspect of general maturity is emotional maturity,

which boils down to an ability to form relationships with other people. Through our emotions we discover that the fulfilment of our personality can come about only in relation to other people, that our nature is essentially social. So we should ask ourselves how sociable we are inclined to be, and whether we find extreme difficulty in talking openly about ourselves to other people. When are are in a group, do we tend to cut ourselves off and create a world of our own? Conversely, our capacity for relationships can also be tested by our capacity for solitude; while some people isolate themselves too much, others are incapable of remaining alone with themselves and with God. They must always have company, whatever they are doing. This is not forming relationships with other people, but being dependent on them, and living only through them, like parasites. That is not maturity.

The sexual aspect of our emotions has a vital influence on our personality as it forms and matures. Sexuality is not a secondary matter but the most sensitive guide to the basic tendencies of each individual. The Bible shows sex as one of the original dimensions in the make-up of God's creatures. 'God created human beings in his own image . . . male and female he created them.' Our sexuality is at the very root of personal and social life, and if properly incorporated can contribute to the making of a balanced man or woman, but if badly adjusted or abused becomes a highly destructive force.

To go more deeply into this important subject would be beyond the scope of this book, but at the risk of being too schematic, let us remember that sexuality must not be reduced to its genital, or mechanical component, which is active for example in sexual intercourse or in masturbation.

116

Sexuality extends far beyond purely genital acts. It is the masculine or feminine dimension which runs through the whole being of the individual from the moment of conception. Every relationship between human beings and things, and between people and God, has a sexual ingredient, though not necessarily genital. All our desires are marked by our experience of sexuality since infancy. Even our life of prayer, our way of seeing God, our apostolic work, are coloured by the way we come to terms with sex.

A person is mature enough for marriage or for virginity if he or she has successfully outgrown two forms of sexual immaturity − narcissism and homosexuality − in order to attain heterosexuality. The child, after feeling the attraction of his own body, discovers an interest in the other person who is not too different from himself; this is called the undifferentiated phase, when homosexuality is dominant (at the level of impulse, not behaviour). From that time onwards the human being learns gradually to accept and love the other person as different, and will eventually find in heterosexual love the fulfilment of his or her desire.

It would be a useful exercise to examine ourselves about our knowledge of sexual matters. What were we taught about it, and how? Was it from our parents or school friends? Did we read any books about it? Did we ever talk openly with anyone about it, especially during our adolescence? How did we get on during puberty and how did we overcome the difficulty of autoeroticism? Did we ask ourselves about the meaning of marriage, and what the union of man and woman signifies in God's plan? We ought also to bear in mind that some adults preserve the traces of narcissism or homosexuality left over from childhood.

The important thing is not to foster any such tendency by forming friendships which are too exclusive and liable to become falsely sentimental. The best foundation for a stable personality is to be sufficiently developed in a consistently heterosexual direction, and this is especially important for people vowed to celibacy. Where heterosexuality cannot be fully expressed, any tendency to homosexuality, narcissism or autoeroticism is in danger of being heightened.

The second stage of sexual development is the gradual passage from self-regarding to self-giving love, and how well this is accomplished will affect the whole personality in its growth to maturity. Sexuality will then be thoroughly blended in the whole person, making its presence known by a capacity for unselfishness, so that we can freely enter into relationships and serious commitments. Our ability to be faithful to our commitments will depend on the self-control we can exercise over that combination of desires, urges, thoughts and habits within us, which make us the person we are. Self-control is another indication of a person's maturity.

All human activity results from internal conflict and tension, which we must learn to control and organize according to a ruling principle of behaviour. Our higher ideals are always at war with our natural instincts, but as these contradictory forces are gradually reconciled, our personality reaches maturity. It is hard enough to accept discipline from an external authority, but when we have learnt to do this and even make the discipline our own, interiorize it, we shall be well on the way to being mature enough to be faithful to our commitments.

Self-control is not restrictive or frustrating. It is simply knowing how to say no, being able to keep faith with our ideals when we are tested, so that all our possibilities, creative, emotional and intellectual can be fulfilled and our true personality can unfold according to its inner principle. Self-control channels our inner energies, and does not block them; it synthesizes contradictory forces and brings about an agreement, in order to avoid an explosion. When all our desires, impulses and thoughts have been channelled and redirected unselfishly our life becomes a continuous and unique act of love.

Whilst on the subject of unselfishness we should ask ourselves whether we usually try to keep out of sight when sacrifices are being called for. How good are we at sticking to a rule of life, and do we live in an orderly fashion, with hours allotted to sleep and work? Do we honour our agreements? Do we have fits of temper, or take irrational decisions on the spur of the moment? Do we disrupt our family life by going off on our own for long periods?

There is another indication of maturity, which cannot be considered in isolation, but without which all the other indications we have mentioned will be of no use for our vocation: it is religious maturity, or the capacity for fellowship with God. Human maturity may enable us to achieve great things, but will do nothing to prepare us for the call to follow Jesus for the sake of the kingdom of heaven. For that we shall need the strength that comes from fellowship with God based on prayer and meditation, which is conversation with the Person, or three Persons, dwelling within us.

Religious maturity, like emotional maturity, is acquired only gradually, and it is gained by attending carefully to our relationship with God. As the divine life extends through our personality it drives us outwards towards others in love which is disinterested, self-offering and capable of suffering. This is the supernatural counterpart of the natural movement from self-regarding to self-giving love. Religious maturity is therefore the fulfilment towards which our true human maturity is always tending; if we are religiously mature we know for certain that we are truly mature as a human being.

Religious maturity brings with it the power of discernment, which is the equivalent, in the new person, of common sense. It is the enlightenment and strengthening of his or her mind by the Holy Spirit. Discernment, like all human capacities, is also acquired gradually, and only if we have interior freedom. For how can God speak to us if we have already made up our minds about everything?

For discernment to work we must listen to God when he speaks, ask him sincerely to tell us what he wants of us, and be ready to welcome his reply with a glad heart. He must say to us what he wants, and we must want what he says. We must therefore be ready for change; willing to reconsider some of our choices and preferences, some of the things we are certain about, but have not been ratified by God. The good that God does not want is an evil. The spirit of evil is just as pleased if a lesser good is performed instead of the greater, as he is with a downright evil. When we choose how we are going to spend our adult life it is essential not to be confused between the greater and lesser goods. Lucifer, the angel of light, will try to dazzle and delude us, and if we lack discernment he will succeed.

XXXVI
The Stages of Discernment

E very man and every woman can be called by God
to some particular service, and being open to this
possibility is the most important thing there is. The normal
course of life will not by itself lead us to our divine vocation,
because we are free, and God so respects our freedom
that he will not approach us directly and ask us to follow
him. If he told us point blank to follow him, should we
have enough independence to refuse, knowing that he is
all-powerful? No, his is a love which seeks in return a love
from us that is sincere and disinterested, and free from any
pressure. He wants us as friends, not frightened servants. If
we wish to know what to do, we must take the initiative,
and use our freedom to approach him, and ask him to tell
us clearly. If we have got that far, then already we must have
chosen God and put everything else in second place. For
before he can call us to share his risen life, God needs to
know that we have chosen him for his own sake, out of
pure love, that is, in the appearance of the wretched and
repellent form of the Crucified.

God is diffident; it is up to us to make him answer, and he
will not be bold enough to reply unless he can be sure that

we shall not refuse him. We remember how the rich young man, after refusing to follow Jesus, went away sorrowful. Those who have heard the call and have not followed him will always retain a certain sadness in their heart of hearts, a longing for another life once glimpsed but rejected. For this loss there is no consolation in any other person, even less in this world's goods, however great they might be, for the greatest good of all has been given in exchange. The call planted in them a capacity for life, love and joy, and suffering – nothing will make up for this. Only God can console them, for his pity is as great as the riches they have lost by their lack of generosity. At the moment when the choice is made we are perfectly free. God gives us to understand that he will never be severe with us for making a choice different from the one he indicated, and that in any case he will still be willing to share our life. He will come to live our life, even if we refuse to live his. He will desire what we desire, even though we refuse what he, who knows us better than we know ourselves, desires for us.

If we are sure of God's love for us and ready to share his life, the great choice we must make first is, marriage or celibacy? Statistically it is much more likely that we are called to marriage, but we shall not be quite sure unless we risk finding out whether God has granted us the gift of virginity and whether therefore he may be calling us to celibacy. If we discern within ourselves the capacity to live in perfect chastity, we probably have a vocation for it. But how can we be sure? Here is a test that will help us to decide. We have within us a double call to infinite love. We are aware on the one hand of a desire for an absolute love, and on the other hand a desire for a love that is universal. We wish to love with all our heart and strength and mind, and we also wish to love everybody. Absolute love can be realized only in marriage, universal love only in virginity; they are mutually exclusive. But both are in the image of God, who is universal love, and yet manages to be absolute for each individual. The choice between marriage and celibacy is, among other things, a choice between these two loves which in this life cannot be reconciled. Each bears the mark of the infinite, but each is marked by the renunciation of another infinite value.

To choose between marriage and celibacy is to acknowledge humbly that one of these loves is beyond our reach for the time being, and must therefore be sacrificed, great as the loss is, but we also know that, by means of the love which we actually enjoy, God is preparing us throughout our life to enjoy his love in its fullness. Those persons whom God calls to marriage, if they are honest with themselves, recognize that true happiness is impossible without the ability to give and receive that kind of love which engages every part of the personality, including especially the aspect of sexuality. Whereas those persons called to virginity recognize that for them the restrictions of a natural family would be intolerable, and that true happiness would be unattainable in the giving and receiving of love with one other person. That way of being faithful would, for that person, be a burden too heavy to bear, just as continence and the renunciation of loved ones would be intolerable for the other. In heaven we shall be able to love universally and absolutely, but on earth we have to choose between them. We are actually so constituted that if we look honestly at ourselves we shall be able to see which kind of love we are intended for, then we can make our choice in peace.

So it has to be one of two things: either we are called to marriage or we are called to virginity. If marriage is our vocation let us live peacefully according to God's will in the present moment, loving our neighbour. One day we shall become aware that one particular neighbour of the opposite sex has captured a special place in our heart. Have we found our soul mate? Why not? Let us just hope, and time will tell. Then through the love for one person we shall increasingly discover what it means to love the whole of humankind. Nothing is small which is done for love, and because love is not divided, the absolute brings us to the universal.

If we are called to virginity, we must decide where to live it, in which Church, if I may so express it. Here too we are faced with a choice which will cause some pain, for it means sacrificing a godly ambition. There are two dimensions to the Church: it is universal, and it is local. In practice these two have given rise to two sorts of membership, two types of vocation to virginity, one displaying more the universality of the Church, the other its rootedness in a particular human community.

The call to serve the local Church has all the appeal of continuity, perseverance, and the involvement of the Church at the very heart of people's lives. Parish priests share in all the joys and sorrows of their people. They witness the birth and growth of children; they marry them, and baptize the new generation. They bring their parishioners to birth in the faith, and accompany them, their children in Christ, along life's journey. It is they to whom people instinctively turn in times of trial, sure of finding understanding and consolation. They are the shepherds who know their sheep, and whose sheep know them, and if only they are faithful to their vocation their parishes are transformed little by little into a bit of paradise on earth. Priests, like the Curé d'Ars, who did not move from his village during his whole life, could boast like him that their graveyards were full of saints. But how many years did it take him to overcome mistrust and conquer the hearts of his parishioners one by one, remaining faithful to them until death?

Because the Church is universal, individuals are called to highlight particular truths of the gospel for the good of the whole Church. So it was with Francis of Assisi and poverty, Teresa of Avila and prayer, Vincent de Paul and practical charity, Alphonse de Liguori and the awareness of the Will of God, Thérèse of Lisieux and the Little Way of total abandonment to the Father. As we study the saints we see that each is like a word or a deed from the gospel underlined, multiplied almost infinitely, incarnate, so to speak, in this saint and the spiritual family which continues in the life and teachings of its founder. 'Blessed are the poor in spirit,' Francis and his Franciscans seem to say. 'Suffer the little children to come to me,' say John Bosco and his teaching congregations untiringly. Vincent de Paul emphasizes the primacy of charity, and Teresa of Avila that of prayer. The Sisters of Bethany, of Bethlehem and of Nazareth, evoke the holy places of the New Testament. The orders of Hospitallers, the contemplatives, the preaching friars – each group reflects in every age and in every part of the earth a gesture, an attitude, a feeling, a word of Jesus. Considering the incredible diversity of the Church's spiritual gifts, we could without any doubt write a large part of the gospel over again. Throughout the Church's history new saints in every generation, approaching the gospel freshly, give it a different emphasis and illuminate it with a new light, so that the message seems like one hitherto unpublished. Time and again the truth is demonstrated that the gospel, the account of the life of God made human, is an inexhaustible treasure and a spring that never runs dry. To bear fruit, we must be grafted on to Christ, on to the Church, according to our vocation. The grafting is achieved either by obedience to the bishop of the local Church to which we belong, or by joining a spiritual family which is an incarnation in the universal Church of a word of life, which it utters on behalf of all.

A vocation to a spiritual family demands a readiness to leave one's country, people, and Church of one's upbringing; to become a stranger in one's own land and a citizen of any other, and an active member of any other local Church, wherever the spiritual gift needs to be carried. The person called to virginity must find out with whom the consecrated life is to be lived, where the grafting on to the Church is to take place, and to whom to be obedient. For in the Christian life obedience is a privilege. It is not a passive or servile obedience; it is the guarantee that we are doing what we really want to do – the will of God. The first hermits who retired from the world and renounced everything soon realized that their egos had gone with them into the desert and, in short, they were following their own inclinations. So they chose one of themselves, a monk who showed signs of wisdom and holiness, and promised obedience to him, and thus was born the monastic life which was to flourish so marvellously thereafter. The person called to virginity is trying to acquire the capacity for poverty, chastity and obedience, and this is possible only in the Church, in a spiritual family.

When we set out to live according to the gospel, such is the severity of the demands of the spiritual life that, unless someone in the community exercises authority over us, our resistance will soon be worn down. Either we shall very soon be discouraged and give up, or else we shall rapidly destroy ourselves in an excess of zeal. The Christian life is not meant to be lived alone. It can only be lived in company with others who, feeling responsible for us, restrain or encourage us in our self-offering. The Christian life urges us to love with all our heart, with all our strength and with all our mind, but we cannot keep this up for long unless our love is returned, and unless we perceive this exchange as the commandment of Jesus, 'Love one another as I have loved you.' But then love can be without limit, the self-giving total, the generosity without restraint. And the love of the others for us will be our safeguard, because they will set limits to our self-giving. They will remind us that the diverse demands of the Christian life are often contradictory.

The first attempts at regulating the life of people consecrated to God resulted in monastic rules, of which the best known and perhaps the most complete and the most balanced is that of St Benedict. We must never forget that the purpose of these rules is to enable monastic communities to follow their vocation. The rule, far from being a meticulous legal code, provides the religious with the right conditions for living according to the call that they have received, and therefore according to their true personalities. Far from being a yoke, it is what secures their freedom and allows them to grow. Just as obedience is the guarantee of freedom, chastity is the guarantee of being able to love everybody, and poverty is the guarantee of being able to enjoy the gifts of the Creator, whose love for us as human beings is unlimited. The poor in the gospel sense learn that there is more joy in giving than in receiving, and that God loves a cheerful giver. Besides, the richest is not the one who amasses the most wealth, but the one whom we feel able to ask for help. So the Counsels of Perfection, as they are called, must be considered in the light of their purpose. Poverty, chastity and obedience are what Jesus proposes; he is not concerned with vices. In any case, wealth, sexuality, self-assertion . . . we know without being told. Jesus is offering us something different: the challenge of the alternative, another life, another world.

Once everything is clear and we know which saint or which bishop to commit ourself to, the only thing left to do is to say 'yes' to God's call, and it all begins. How we wish we knew what Jesus had in store for us as we follow him! Fortunately, we know nothing. Only one thing is certain, and that is that we shall die like everyone else after having our share of joy and suffering. More than the others? I doubt it. Different, perhaps. The saints give the impression that their experience of joy and suffering was more intense. They did not rail against suffering and they welcomed life's joys with simplicity. They laughed and they wept like children. Their consolations, like their trials, were extreme. More than anyone else, the saints seem to have really lived.